{ The Gratitude Attitude }

The Gratitude Attitude

A Joyful Christian's Guide
to Living More Richly with Less

David & Lo-Ann Trembley

ZONDERVAN

GRAND RAPIDS, MICHIGAN 49530 USA

ZONDERVAN™

The Gratitude Attitude
Copyright © 2003 by David and Lo-Ann Trembley

Requests for information should be addressed to:
Zondervan, *Grand Rapids, Michigan 49530*

Library of Congress Cataloging-in-Publication Data

Trembley, David.
    The gratitude attitude : a joyful Christian's guide to living more richly with less / David and Lo-Ann Trembley.
       p. cm.
    ISBN 0-310-24827-2
    1. Christian life — Meditations.   2. Gratitude — Religious aspects — Christianity.   I. Trembley, Lo-Ann. II. Title.
    BV4501.3 .T73   2003
    242 — dc21

2002155549

All Scripture quotations, unless otherwise indicated, are taken from the *Holy Bible: New International Version*®. NIV®. Copyright © 1973, 1978, 1984 by International Bible Society. Used by permission of Zondervan. All rights reserved.

All rights reserved. No part of this publication may be reproduced, stored in a retrieval system, or transmitted in any form or by any means — electronic, mechanical, photocopy, recording, or any other — except for brief quotations in printed reviews, without the prior permission of the publisher.

Interior design by Beth Shagene

Printed in the United States of America

---

03 04 05 06 07 08 09 10 /❖ DC/ 10 9 8 7 6 5 4 3 2 1

Preface

Do you remember when you were a kid and the grown-ups told you, "Say thank you"? You had to say it. Sometimes you had to say thank you for something you really didn't want or even like. "Say thank you to Aunt Rose for that nice pair of brown socks." Everybody's eyes were on you and you felt like disappearing (if only you could), so you'd drop your head and mumble the words into your chest.

Since they were muffled into your shirt front, they came out sounding like "Thin goo."

Eventually, the "thank you" became ingrained so that now, if you're at all like me, you say "thank you" almost automatically.

"Your bill comes to $2,374.39."

"Thank you."

"Hi, how are you today. I'm calling with a special offer for gutter and downspout replacement."

"Thank you. We're not interested."

"Looks like you're going to need a root canal."

"Thank you."

Preface

By grace, we move beyond this kind of thank-you. By grace, we find our way to the gratitude attitude that is beyond polite formulas and springs up from the heart as a burst of joy, not an automatic reflex. When we are at our childlike best, our thank-yous burst from us with exuberance. "Oh, thank you! I love it." Nobody has to tell us to say the words. If anything, we don't have enough or the right kinds of words to express just how pleased and delighted we are.

That kind of overflowing joy is what gospel living is all about. We wrote this book because we hope to share some of the ways we have become aware of God's blessing in our lives. By sharing our experiences, we hope you will discover more of your own. "Count your blessings," says the old hymn. "Name them one by one, and you will discover what our God has done." *The Gratitude Attitude* is our way of taking an inventory of God's grace active in our lives. We didn't make it. We can't take credit. Grace happens!

We can no more control grace than choose the color of our eyes or the day we were born. We can, however, cooperate with grace in our lives to make the most of who we were meant to be. The old Mother Goose rhyme says,

Monday's child is fair of face;
Tuesday's child is full of grace;
Wednesday's child is full of woe;
Thursday's child has far to go;
Friday's child is loving and giving;
Saturday's child works hard for a living.
But the child born on the Sabbath day
Is bright and blithe and bonny and gay.

Preface

We didn't choose the day we were born. We can accept or reject the "fortune" associated with that day. The rhyme isn't really a prognostication of our fate but a reminder. Although we all have only seven days in each week, how we use those days is up to us. There is a broad spectrum of potential responses from living as a victim "full of woe" to living as a victor with more than enough to be "loving and giving."

This old rhyme seems to capture so well the range of human experience that we used it to organize the meditations of this book. Each of the seven days has nine short essays that reflect on the theme for that day. With each devotion we suggest a Scripture reading that is, in some way, "in conversation" with the meditation. The Scripture in one way or another rounds out, resolves, or enriches the essay's point. We conclude each devotion with a brief prayer—often of gratitude—because God is *so* good.

How we arranged the material is one thing. How you use the material is another. You can read sequentially for nine weeks, proceeding day by day; or you can skip around reading what strikes your fancy, following the Spirit's lead. Don't feel constrained by our scheme. After all, if it means anything, a gratitude attitude means living filled with freedom, joy, and delight.

Finally, writing this book is only half the dialog. If something you read triggers a response that you would like to share, we are eager to hear from you. We can be reached at

TheGratAtt@aol.com

Thank you for your interest (as buyer, reader, or gift giver) in this book. You are, whether you know it or not, one reason for *The Gratitude Attitude* in these authors' lives.

David and Lo-Ann Trembley
Summer 2002

Monday's child is fair of face.

Monday

Monster in the Pot

Acts 10:9–15

I don't know what prompted my decision to buy *pulpo*. Say it was that the Hispanic *supermarcado* offered a special. Say it was my taste for exotic food or my adventurous spirit as a cook. Say it was that after almost twenty-five years of marriage I know my spouse likes food with resistance. Say whatever you like. I bought some.

Pulpo comes in a frozen chunk about the color, shape, and size of a paving block, one of the round ones people use in their gardens. Although my friend Gregorio, who happens to be both Hispanic and a cook, has mentioned his affection for *pulpo*, he has never told me how he prepares it.

Not to worry! Boiling, I decide, is the safest course. I will put my *pulpo* in the pot and at the very least thaw it out. Later I can decide what to do with it. I am, however, already imagining *pulpo* with tomatoes, onion, and green peppers over pasta. I put the pot on to boil and go about other chores. After what I consider adequate time, I check on the progress of my *pulpo*. I don't know what I expect, but it isn't what I get.

Monday's child is fair of face.

I lift the lid to take a peek. Staring back at me from stygian blackness is an alien from a sci-fi movie. A monstrous bobbling head with googly eyes glowers at me. I scream and slam down the lid. My heart pounding, I back away as if the creature were about to attack.

When I recover sufficiently, my hand still shaking, I lift the lid. *Pulpo* is Spanish for "octopus." When it thawed, the octopus returned to its original shape and released its ink. There in the pot is a bulbous head afloat in black water, its eyes blank discs. I gather my addled wits and begin reasoning with myself. I try to remember from high school biology everything I know about octopus anatomy.

"Look, it's just cooked," I reassure myself. "You've cleaned fish before. It can't be any worse than that." With a shudder, I scoop the creature from the water. With fainthearted delicacy, I turn my head away and decapitate the beast. My squeamishness returns. I am both fascinated and repulsed by the parrot-like beak at the base of the balloon head. What remains is a tangled mass of tentacles resembling a cheap hairpiece. The tentacle tips extend outward until they are pencil-point thin. The suction cups diminish in size like a study in perspective. I suddenly find myself marveling at this primitive wonder from the sea.

These cupules are a problem I hadn't anticipated. The last time I ate calamari I didn't notice any suckers left on the meat. How does one remove them? Scrape them? Strip them? Slice them? Tentatively, I run a tentacle through my fingers as though stripping leaves from a stem. The suction cups and skin peel cleanly away.

Monday's child is fair of face.

The excitement is over. The rest of the chopping, stewing, and serving follows culinary convention. My spouse is delighted with the finished dish, as am I. The *pulpo* is a success. I must nevertheless confess that it has taken me nearly a year to dare buying more *pulpo*, but we do have another paving block in the freezer waiting to be dropped into the pot.

> *Thank you, dear God, that you have created such varied creatures. Open us to the wonder of your world. Teach us to appreciate each little adventure and discovery that come our way. Amen.*

Tuesday

Tuesday's child is full of grace.

Awaking to Luxury

JOHN 5:2–9A

Twenty- and thirty-somethings will have a hard time believing it, but the day is coming when it will no longer be possible to bounce out of bed. The bounce will become more like a hoisting, and then many joints will complain during the journey downstairs.

Let us now consider the possibilities of remediation. We could move to Arizona. Dry heat, they tell us, is good for arthritis. I've seen a new medication advertised that promises to dispense with arthritis pain. I don't know how expensive it is, but I did read the small print, and there is mention of potential liver damage. I think I would rather ache.

I wonder if it would be possible to hire a personal trainer and masseuse. A house call would probably cost about a hundred fifty dollars, and I need these services at least five times a week, so I might as well make this person a live-in employee and give him or her other things to do after our morning exercises are over. (I wonder if a masseuse would be willing also to run the vacuum and wash the windows.)

Tuesday's child is full of grace.

Now that I've put my mind to it, I see that there are many solutions. One is an in-home pool. Of course, it would mean substantial reconstruction of the house. We might be better off simply moving.

Wait a minute! I've just had an inspiration. Exactly what I need for my fifty-something ailments is already installed in my home. All I must do is access it. I step into the cubical, slide shut the door, and, *voilà!* Instant hydrotherapy. I stand beneath my shower, turn up the hot, breathe in the steamy air, and marvel at my blessing. What proportion of all the human beings who have ever lived have water piped into their houses, much less hot water? Heat, water, light, and electric power are all mine with the flip of my wrist.

I have slept the night snug in a bed more comfortable than the vast majority of humankind has ever known. I have been safe behind locked doors, with a telephone at hand ready to summon a vast variety of aid should I need it. I make my morning coffee and cook my breakfast using tools that are designed to produce life's little luxuries with virtually no effort from me. Now I stand beneath this pulsating throb of hot water washing away the stiffness of the night, and I wonder.

How could I think myself anything other than rich? I will shortly pick from a closet full of clothes, walk to the garage, press the button that opens the door I do not even have to lift for myself, and drive away in my own personal automobile. The great likelihood is that I shall do pretty much what I want today and then come home to comfort and ease.

In the middle of all this wealth, it astonishes me to remember that, according to the economic standards of USAmerica, we are living on the edge of poverty. Although guilt is not one of my

Tuesday's child is full of grace.

favorite things, I confess to an awareness of guilt this morning. To think that I have ever complained that I do not have enough. That I want—even "need"—more!

It must be time to pray!

> *Lord Jesus, forgive me for my obliviousness. Thank you for this shocking reminder of my blessedness. Teach me, merciful Savior, to live in thanksgiving and joy. Amen.*

Wednesday's child is full of woe.   **Wednesday**

Rise and Shine

Isaiah 60:1 – 5

I'm stumped. What's the matter with me? Earlier today I played two-suit spider solitaire—and won. Now, just a few hours later, I can't do anything right. My eyes are burning, the cards go out of focus, and I can feel a headache coming on. I thought I had this game figured out. Well, duh! I've worked hard all day; I'm tired. End of mystery; it's time for bed.

I've been reading in the news lately that USAmerica is a nation sadly under-slept. We go to bed too late, rise too early, and walk through the day half numb. It's a sign of our having too much to do, some claim. It's a mark of how engaged we are in life, but I'm not so sure. I think the deep explanation is almost exactly the opposite.

Habitual tiredness, I think, is no mere byproduct of other choices. Indeed, I believe it is, perhaps not quite consciously, purposeful. I think we accomplish the same thing with being weary that we accomplish with nicotine, alcohol, and other substance abuse. In short, we dull ourselves because it is frightening to be fully alive, and frightening to admit we won't always be.

Wednesday's child is full of woe.

One response to the dark side of life is to deny it. Don't air your dirty linen in public, keep it in the family, don't talk about it, look at the bright side, the glass is half full—these are typical expressions of the insistence that every day, in every way, life is getting better and better.

But there is a dark side to our lives. Freudians call it the death wish; Jungians call it the life of the shadow. The biblical terminology is "the way of the flesh" and "bondage to sin and death." Whatever we call it, the truth is we human beings are all conflicted. We are ambivalent and ambiguous. We are drawn to evil and death as well as life and good. In this world, nothing is entirely good, and nothing is perfectly evil. Dealing with our attraction to darkness begins with naming and exploring this pervasive ambiguity.

I know people, for example, who bewail the need for sleep. They force themselves to have as few hours as they can possibly manage of slumber and then work as hard as they can until, typically, they get so tired they crash or so ill they must go to bed. But rest is part of life. Sleep is not the enemy. Productivity is not the only thing that matters. It is just as vital for us to be as it is to do.

Indeed, overemphasis upon productivity may signal very serious soul sickness. Our "work" may well be an attempt at works righteousness. We may be trying not only to distract ourselves from the quiet that unsettles us but actually trying to earn our way into heaven. It is not possible of course, but we may be running so fast and becoming so weary precisely to avoid seeing the impossibility.

The counsel of Jesus is very instructive. Take no thought for tomorrow; consider the lilies of the field. What person can by

Wednesday's child is full of woe.

merely thinking about it add an inch to height or a second to life? Truly, a righteous life is a life of right rhythm. The world turns, and the sun rises and sets. The seasons pass and the years. In all of it, the parts we like and the parts we do not, it is possible to see the presence of God. But sometimes it means slowing down, dropping what we are doing, and getting a good night's sleep.

> *Thank you for life's rhythms, dear God.*
> *Tune us to them so that we might move at your pace*
> *in your direction, in imitation of your Son. Amen.*

Thursday

Thursday's child has far to go.

Schedule Your Day

ECCLESIASTES 3:1–13

What's this? Too busy? Not enough time? We all live twenty-four-hour days, but sometimes we do not use those hours effectively. *Tempus fugit*, but this time with a twist. Rest assured, no great cosmic issues will sneak into this conversation. Our topic is much more limited, just the twenty-four hours of today.

A daily list reminds us of our priorities. We human beings are lazy and tempted to avoid clarity, but clarity is good for us. So we suggest writing a daily to-do list. The writing itself provides us insight even if we don't pay any attention to the list after we have written it. Just writing encourages us to get clearer about our priorities. Creating our list also helps us strategize more effective use of our time and resources to realize those priorities.

We suggest two organizational schemes for these daily lists. The first is chronological. Whatever is important enough to set a time for is probably important enough to do. In fact, setting a specific time is a safeguard for determining whether the activity matters to us. When we write it down, we form a mental contract

Thursday's child has far to go.

with ourselves. The written-down agenda item has a tangibility that distinguishes it from mere vague good intentions. For instance, Lo-Ann hates to market her writing, but when she finally makes a list of potential publishers, I know she is serious about sending off her material.

The second organizational scheme is order of importance. Rank the items with the most important thing at the top of the list and the least at the bottom. If you want to quit here, you will probably have profited from the exercise. If you intend actually to use your list, however, we have some more suggestions.

Start each day with a clean slate. Don't automatically carry over items from one day to the next. Instead, think about each item before writing it down. Do you really want to do this thing? Secondly, consider saving your lists for a while and looking back at them. You may discover that the same items or the same kinds of items keep not being done day after day. If this is your discovery, perhaps you can learn why these items get avoided. Whose agenda are they anyway?

Thirdly, are there some items that you really care about, but they are too much to deal with in a single day? If so, break your big goals into manageable chunks. For example, if I compose just one page a day, I will have a book-length manuscript by the end of the year. It might be very interesting to save your lists for some months, perhaps even a year. You will discover both how you are changing and whether you are growing according to plan.

In our household, we have two distinct styles of list making. I have daily slips of paper with itemized entries. Lo-Ann creates and revises her lists in her journal. My lists are task specific, but hers are impressionistic, broad-stroke goal statements. We are each committed to our own approach to list making, yet

Thursday's child has far to go.

both styles provide a checkable indication of personal development.

Finally, think about using these lists for serious reflection. If you share your lists with your spouse, close friends, and God, you may make some surprising progress. I recently was fussing about not accomplishing enough and wasting too much time. Then I reviewed my lists as part of my prayer time. I heard God reminding me of my need to stop my excessive focus upon productivity in order to sometimes simply be.

What's that? You say we misled you about not letting cosmic issues sneak into this discussion? Yes, I guess we did. That's one of the most uncomfortable things about cosmic issues: they are always present whether or not we notice.

> *What a wonderful gift time is, dear God. Thank you for our limits. Thank you that we get to choose what to do and when to do it. Amen.*

Friday's child is loving and giving. # Friday

A Breath of Fresh Air

GENESIS 2:7

We have a confession. Last summer we installed air-conditioning. We just couldn't bear another summer of being unable to breathe. The year before, one of us went down to the basement and threatened not to come up until September. Yesterday it was 85 and humid, so we turned on the air-conditioning, but in the evening we opened the doors and windows to let the fresh air blow through.

We're living proof of that human truth: If we have it, we use it. Think about CBs. At first only semi drivers had them; then they spread to automobiles. Once only doctors had pagers; now it seems that every teenager has an ear glued to a cell phone. People use them everywhere constantly—while driving, during meals in restaurants, and even at the symphony. So it is with our air-conditioning. We want to keep our use to a minimum, but that intention requires constant monitoring. Now that we have it, should we use it?

After all, air-conditioning is expensive. In addition to the substantial purchase price, the energy costs go on and on. There

Friday's child is loving and giving.

are other costs as well. Our artificial, air-conditioned environment threatens to turn us into hothouse flowers. The truth is that life is better without air-conditioning. The closed and sealed windows and soft hum separate us from the world.

In the olden days wide shady porches cooled air that passed through open windows. Cross ventilation kept air moving. Fans were handheld woven palm fronds. Cooling was done with tall glasses of ice-cold lemonade. People passed the time of day commiserating with one another about the heat.

"Hot enough for you?"

"I'll say! I can't remember it being this hot last summer."

Folks with air-conditioning stay indoors. We hurry from our air-conditioned homes to our air-conditioned cars so that we can rush from the parking lot to our air-conditioned jobs. Our lungs long for the breath of life. We are part of a natural order. When we insulate ourselves from our creatureliness, we often pay prices that we do not even recognize, much less intend. For the sake of comfort, we disconnect from each other and our world.

We have to chuckle at the irony that on the very worst, the very hottest days of summer, we probably won't be able to use our air conditioner anyway. Every summer the brownouts and blackouts hit. The electric company says, "Turn off your air conditioner. Go to the mall to cool off." In spite of ourselves, we will be obliged to discover those elusive, inexpensive alternatives to air-conditioning. We could go outside—to the beach, a park, or to sit under a tree. The air outside is fresh, not recycled, and so inviting. How eager we are to breathe deeply of life's energy. So on those days when asthma and allergies permit, we promise to . . .

Friday's child is loving and giving.

- enjoy the heat we yearned for standing knee-deep in snow;
- stay outside as much as we can and sweat with impunity;
- share a cool drink and a leisurely chat with a neighbor while we wait together for that first cool evening breeze.

> *Thank you, God, that we still have the sense sometimes to stop and take a deep breath and experience how good your creation is. Thank you for the human ingenuity that tinkers and fixes and for the wisdom that tells us when to leave well enough alone. Amen.*

Saturday

Saturday's child works hard for a living.

Take a Vocation

FIRST CORINTHIANS 7:17–24

What is the relationship between work and play? What should that relationship be?

I first asked these questions in my early twenties. I was standing in the empty classroom, after the first week of teaching and saying aloud, "Are they really paying me for this? I would gladly pay them."

Teachers are not the only ones who love their work. Four or five weeks ago the church van broke down, and Joe, from Road Patrol, arrived. His spotless black-and-white truck was highly polished, he quickly began hooking up the chains, and soon we were off.

Riding north on Seventeenth Street, just to make conversation, I said to Joe, "Gee, this must be a boring job."

Joe looked at me as if I were crazy. He almost lost control of the truck.

"Boring!" Joe said. "Not at all. What makes you think so? Why, I could tell you stories . . . ," and he proceeded to tell a story or two. He told about running on the shoulder of I–43 with his

Saturday's child works hard for a living.

lights flashing and everyone making way. He told of the medical evacuation helicopter landing within thirty feet of his truck. He told proudly of the expertise required to right an overturned car thereby getting the lanes free and traffic moving again.

"Boring," Joe said. "Not a bit. I've been driving tow truck for seventeen years now, and I've never been bored. I love this job."

Many people do not love their jobs. In fact, they can barely tolerate what they do for a living. Of course, there is complaining that is only disguised bragging, but many people are positively miserable at work. There seems to be no direct connection between the amount of misery they experience and the kind of work they do.

Jolly and grim pastors, happy and wretched painters, restless and satisfied sales clerks—job satisfaction comes in all shapes and sizes. The key ingredient seems simply to be, is this person doing what he or she is meant to do? Job satisfaction is not so much a "what" as a "how." For people who love their jobs, the distinction between work and play is very subtle. The middle of a work day is just as satisfying as a day of vacation because one is engaged in a vocation, but many folks don't have vocations or even careers; they just have jobs.

You sometimes can tell the difference on first meeting. The certified nursing assistants at Westshore Nursing Home provide a good example. Among the CNAs are some whose vocation is care giving. They virtually adopt the patients in their care. Every act—bathing, feeding, toileting—is ministry. Others who are merely working in the facility, sneak off to the break room, gossip in the hall, or do anything they can to avoid patient contact. The first group personifies the satisfactions of vocation; they are doing what they are called to do. The second embodies the vexation of holding down a job; they work because they must.

Saturday's child works hard for a living.

Each of us has our own calling. Our true work is as unique as our gifts. I was surprised at Joe's job satisfaction. Others, like Zack, are equally astonished by mine. Zack is forty-five, drives semis with enviable skill, and has a serious TV addiction. He can't fathom why anyone would read a book, much less write one. When Zack found out we were writing another book, he curled his lip and said, "I just don't get it. What's the fun in that?"

It is near the end of another semester. Thirty-eight years after standing in that first classroom, I still teach. I heard myself saying just the other day, "They pay me for this? I'd gladly pay them."

Meanwhile, Joe, the tow-truck driver, has backed the church van into its space and unhooked all the chains. He reports in on his radio and learns that he has another call waiting, far away on the south side.

"Gotta go," Joe says. "Busy day. God, I love this job!"

> *Thank you, God, for the variety of work. Thank you that there is satisfaction and even joy hiding in the most surprising places. Help us believe that you have particular work for us to do, and then give us the courage to claim it. Amen.*

*But the child born on the Sabbath day
is bright and blithe and bonny and gay.*

Sunday

Doing Church Differently

MATTHEW 25:34 – 36

In our congregation we have three rules. The first is "Do everything from joy and thanksgiving." The second is "Do nothing from guilt or obligation." Our third rule is "Don't tell anyone else what to do." Some folks, when they hear our rules say, "You can't have a church without guilt! Nothing would ever get done."

They have a point. Most folks want and need structure. Guilt is, in fact, the basis of much religious practice. Have you ever heard, for instance, the joke about folks who went to worship to get whipped on Sunday morning so they would be free to sin as usual on Monday afternoon? It is true that our rules mean that our congregation will always be small and marginal, but we nevertheless believe in and cherish the power, freedom, and joy.

Everyone has something to share. Everybody really wants to give. The incredible fact is that when you give of yourself, you always get back more. It's like teaching. You always learn more when you have to teach someone else.

Mother Teresa shows us how. There are incredible joy and

But the child born on the Sabbath day is bright and blithe and bonny and gay.

power in loving the poor, the outcast, and the dying. The poor reveal our rich resources. Outcasts best teach us about the dignity and beauty of each human being. The dying are the true authorities on the importance of living well.

Our potential teachers are all around us. To receive their wisdom, we must first learn from Christ. Paul tells us that Christ emptied himself of divinity in order to assume humanity (Philippians 2:6–7). From strength, Christ chose weakness and vulnerability. Christ could have overwhelmed us with power and majesty. Instead Christ chose to love us. Christ's choice has profound consequences for human relating.

I cannot give of myself unless, and until, I know who my self is. The behaviors I may call "love" are often mere pretext or pretense—an excuse to use others to meet my own needs. Too often, I turn love into a deal. Such pretending depletes rather than fulfills. Christlike loving, however, is not subtraction; it is multiplication. Both giver and receiver are enriched. Indeed, the resulting mutuality so blurs the roles as to make them indistinguishable and irrelevant. Giver gets and getter gives.

Our congregation has a significant contingent of persons who happen to be mentally challenged. People learning of our ministry erroneously respond, "You are doing such a wonderful work. I admire you so." The implication is that we are saintly people to be working with "them," but the truth is we are the ones who are blessed.

"They" have taught us many profound lessons about what loving Jesus really means. We have learned far more about practical theology from our mentally challenged friends than we learned in seminary. Through our relationships we have learned to become more welcoming of all kinds of "others."

But the child born on the Sabbath day is bright and blithe and bonny and gay.

Our church meets in some of the poorest sections of Milwaukee's inner city. In fact, we move around the city. One Sunday we meet in a residential treatment center for folks who happen to be mentally challenged. Another Sunday we meet in the sort of nursing home that you might not want to send your parents to. Twice a month we share the space of a Christian center.

These are not the sorts of places where Christians traditionally gather for worship, but when I look, I see Jesus' face on little Johnny Akers. Eight years old, a speech impediment, certainly learning disabled, Johnny nearly always smells bad. Every time he sees me, he runs from whatever he is doing, leaps into my arms, and gives me a huge hug. As far as I can tell, I have not done anything to improve Johnny's life, yet here in his embrace is an outpouring of unadulterated joy.

Johnny's joy is one of the surest confirmations of the rightness of Broken Walls' rules. He loves from joy and thanksgiving; guilt and obligation are the farthest things from his mind; and he hardly ever tells anyone what to do, but with every hug he proclaims God's great good news.

*Thank you that your mercy is unlimited, dear God.
Thank you that you are everywhere, waiting
to be seen in the most surprising faces and lives.
Thank you most especially that the poor
and hurting are agents of your joy. Amen.*

Monday

Monday's child is fair of face.

Taste for the Finer Things

2 Chronicles 2:13–14

Our living room is filled with crosses. In my mind's eye I can see five of them. There's the one made from a welding rod attached to painted particleboard that we bought from a wild-looking man at the "Starving Artists' Show," a blue and white tin cross that came from the United Community Folk Art Outlet, and a little ornate bronze cross that was a gift from a member of a church I once pastored. The collection is rounded out by a plain cross and a crucifix, one of which came from a thrift store and the other from a flea market.

Crosses are not the only things on our living room walls. Our habit of collecting folk art began one day when we happened into a little import shop because we had arrived early for a movie. It was love at first sight: a mother and child carved from wood, from Sumatra. Part of the fun of buying it was the bargaining, but the truth is we would have paid a good deal more.

The purchase of the Sumatran piece was like the first shifting of snow that starts an avalanche. We now have a number of

Monday's child is fair of face.

little wooden statues, mostly from Africa, a Hmong story cloth, a surreal painting from Haiti, two trays from Mexico, and a plantain collage from Ghana of two women making *fufu* (pounding manioc into flour). It is a most eclectic collection. As far as I can tell, the objects have only three things in common. They are folk art rather than fine art, they are all quite inexpensive, and each one was acquired simply because we felt drawn to it.

Collecting art is a wonderful way to discover how arbitrary money is. What is a particular object worth? The only real answer is "whatever someone is willing to pay." Our art collection forcefully reminds us that financial value and real worth are often not related in any very meaningful way.

With art as with much of life, truly it is a matter of taste. One of the most important questions is, Does desire cause monetary value, or does monetary value cause desire? To answer that question, let's take a closer look at that painting from Haiti hanging in our living room. We have owned the painting for years. We periodically return to it and every time are delighted anew. It is subtle and intriguing and cost us not a single penny. A friend on vacation had purchased it for five dollars from a street vendor. After a while she grew tired of it and was going to put it in the trash. Before she did, however, she said to herself, "I wonder if the Trembleys would enjoy this." They would, and do.

Taste—what is it? "Taste" always means "preference." I like it or I do not like it, and the reasons tell as much about me as they do about the object. Although taste is often associated with the arts, we also have tastes in people, places, and activities as well as in food and drink. Taste can be important in even very practical matters like—well, like refrigerators. A new refrigerator might cost as little as six hundred dollars. Or as much as— the sky really is the limit. Comes then the question: Do you need

Monday's child is fair of face.

a twenty-eight-hundred-dollar refrigerator? Do you even want one? If so, why?

Many folks get trapped into buying more expensive items under the delusion that they are buying higher quality, but really, what do we want our refrigerators to do? We could ask a similar question about every item we might buy.

I collect not only crosses but also chess sets. Two of my sets are relatively expensive, both of bronze, one from Ghana and the other from Kenya. My favorite set, however, and the one that is most artistically interesting, is handmade from clay. How much is it worth? I'll leave it for my heirs to find out, for the set was made for me by a friend who has died, and to me it is absolutely priceless.

Well, not "absolutely" priceless. If someone were to happen into our living room, see that chess set and offer me ten thousand dollars, I would probably say yes. But then I would have to do a good deal of thinking to try to understand why someone had such an intense yearning for this particular chess set.

> *Thank you, God, that you have made the world with so much beauty. Thank you for the freedom and creativity that allow us a part in deciding what is beauty and what is value. Teach us to appraise correctly the treasures of our lives. Amen.*

Tuesday's child is full of grace.

Tuesday

Tourist or Steward?

1 Peter 4:7–11

How do you fit in the world? What is your position, and how are you connected?

Many of us are not ready for these questions because we feel we do not fit in at all. It is as if the world is not our home and we are strangers in a strange land. It is comforting to remember that everyone feels alienated sometimes. Even deeper comfort comes from the ample scriptural warrant for feeling not at home (see especially Hebrews 11:13–16). The truth is that we all both do and do not fit in.

There are people who recognize and even count upon us. There are places that are familiar and where we feel more comfortable than anywhere else. There are activities that seem right to us and make us feel that we really do know what we are doing.

Where are your places? Who are your people? What are your activities?

Since World War II there has been a growing awareness in the United States that we are the "ugly Americans." Why is that? What makes us ugly in the eyes of much of the rest of the world?

Tuesday's child is full of grace.

The word *ugly* sounds so harsh. We don't think of ourselves as ugly, of course, but from the perspective of the Third World, we have too much, use too much, and boss others around way too much. These are the sorts of behaviors that lead much of the world to think of USAmerica as ugly.

We can soften the harshness of the word, perhaps, by remembering that USAmericans have been joined in recent years by "ugly" Japanese, Germans, and even a Russian or two. As the economies of these nations have advanced, some citizens have prospered enough that they have become tourists, and tourism is always ugly. Tourists come to see, not to share. They stand watching rather than ever becoming involved. When tourists have gotten their fill, they go away; they never meant to stay.

No wonder people don't like tourists! They come to play, and that fact doesn't necessarily bother us too much, although we might envy them for not having any work to do. The problem is that we are the toys they play with. We are their objects of amusement and diversion. They don't care about us. When we cease to amuse them, they leave.

Comes now the question, which goes beyond how we behave on vacation. The question is, Are you living your life as tourist or as steward? Are you just watching, or are you involved? Are you merely seeking your own pleasure, or will you stick around a while and do some work?

Yes, life is short. Yes, as Hebrews says, we are pilgrims and sojourners. The earth is not our ultimate home. But it is our home now, and while we are here, we are charged with the responsibility of being stewards. Stewards are not owners. Stewards are not free to do whatever they feel like doing.

Tuesday's child is full of grace.

Stewards are agents of the Owner, charged by the Owner with responsibility to tend to the Owner's interests.

So if we quit acting like tourists and start behaving like stewards, we just might discover that we have found the place where we belong. What corner of the creation might benefit from your attention? What skills, abilities, and talents do you have that might make this world a better place? Tourism, it turns out, is not much fun even for the tourist. Tourists must always anticipate the next diversion because they have no investment in where they are.

Listen to all those "economic" words! Work, responsibility, owner, agent, steward, investment—whether and how we fit in are matters over which we have a significant amount of control. Being a steward means that we belong here. We did not just happen by. We were sent to this place on purpose, and we have work to do. Indeed, stewards and tourists do not even take the same kinds of vacations.

> *Thank you for this creation that you love so much.*
> *Thank you for entrusting us with its care.*
> *Help us find a right measure and*
> *kind of belonging in the world. Amen.*

Wednesday

Wednesday's child is full of woe.

Feeling Our Way

ACTS 5:1–6

Twelve-Step spirituality, one of the most practical forms of Christianity that ever existed, tells us that there are only five feelings: glad, sad, mad, scared, and ashamed. It is very instructive, in some more words borrowed from the Twelve-Steppers, to "conduct a fearless moral inventory," detailing how we feel about money. Here's the beginning of mine.

Money (and the things money can buy) hardly ever makes me glad. I believe myself to be well blessed in this regard, and I remember exactly when the blessing began. I was in my early twenties, nearly finished with my undergraduate degree, and my father said to me, "David, if you ever make $25,000 a year, you will be a rich man."

It was the early 1960s. Twenty-five thousand dollars then seemed like a lot of money. For example, the first year I taught was 1965–66; my salary was $3,600. I therefore had no difficulty at all in sharing my father's idea that an annual income of $25,000 would mean that I was rich and successful.

Wednesday's child is full of woe.

What cured me of my delusions was the "success" that followed. I went into business and achieved the annual income my father had wished for me. In the process, my marriage ended, I was no longer able to be my son's full-time dad, and I became addicted to a variety of chemicals. The experience was very illuminating. Although I was financially successful, I was more personally miserable than ever before. Never since have I ever been able to connect money and gladness.

Indeed, thinking about money often makes me sad. On Easter in 2002, I visited my eighty-three-year-old, wheelchair-bound mother. For most of my life, a visit to my parents resulted, as I was leaving, in their handing me some money. The practice continued long after I had as much money as I needed. "For gas," they would say while handing me the money, or "buy yourself some supper," but the money wasn't really for such mundane things. It was a sign of their nurture and care. For years, the exchange was a kind of loving charade.

In our family, as in many other boomer families, the roles are now reversed. Instead of Mom's handing me money "for gas," I ask, "Is there anything you need?" She allows as how some insulated drapes on the patio door would be nice. Whether or not we get those drapes, neither of us is dealing very well with our role reversal. She still wants to be the giver, and I wish she could be.

And it makes me mad. It is another discovery of the humanistic psychologies: anger and hurt are the opposite sides of the same coin. Scratch hard enough whichever one appears on the surface, and you will make your way to the other.

We don't want to brood on the negativity, but genuine healing often begins with clear naming. Why am I angry? Part of it has to do with the distance between Mom and me. I wish our

Wednesday's child is full of woe.

relationship were so righteous that things like money wouldn't make any difference, but my anger (and the hurt that preceded it) is evidence enough that our relationship is not that righteous. Now what?

I need to go do some spirit work. When I return I can examine how money scares me and makes me ashamed. Meanwhile, would it be a good idea for you to begin your own fearless moral inventory? Discovering and naming how we really feel is often the beginning of authentic change, and I've done enough discovering and naming in this meditation to know what comes next for me. How about you?

> *Thank you for our feelings, dear God. Thank you for the truths they tell and for the possibility of changing. Give us real vision about our emotional connection with money so we can become more righteous stewards. Amen.*

Thursday's child has far to go. **Thursday**

Freestyle

PSALM 8:5 – 9

I once read a book by a woman who went to live with the Amish. Allegedly, the author was seeking to learn the Amish gift for plain and simple living. The only problem with her approach was that she wanted the gift but didn't want to change her life. She wanted the benefits of Amish living while maintaining her life amid complex modernity. She tried to annex their simplicity without considering the implications.

I sympathize. It is difficult to "work out one's salvation with fear and trembling." It's hard to find your own way. I remember a while ago I kept praying for a giant eraser that would wipe out all the unpleasantness from an old painful relationship. I wanted to wash the slate of all its dusty, gritty history. I learned that I am not God who "makes all things new." Instead, I must proceed incrementally. When I let go of the past, I still must forgive each new incident in the present. God can work on a grand scale; my level is the small, niggling, and mundane.

On the whole, it's not such a bad arrangement. The little bits are all I can really handle anyway. The same principle

Thursday's child has far to go.

applies when working toward simplicity. I don't need utterly to revamp my life. If I change piece by small piece; if I am consistent and persistent, eventually the alterations will add up to transformation.

The woman who went to live with the Amish came back home dissatisfied. Since she hadn't converted to Amish belief or way of life, she couldn't appropriate their benefits. She was back at square one, needing to simplify her own life in her own way.

For some, it may be possible to renounce all earthly possessions and enter a hermitage. After all, Jesus did advise the rich young ruler, "Sell all you have and give the proceeds to the poor and then come follow me." The rich young man believed he couldn't, so he didn't.

It's amazing what we can do when we must. *Newsweek* magazine quoted a petite woman who lifted the rear end of a car to free her trapped husband. "It didn't seem heavy," she said. People are able to radically change their diets and lifestyles when it's a matter of life or death.

God gives us incredible power to do and be.

For folks like me, the decision to simplify is undramatic. My conversion began with reading the *More with Less Cookbook* (Herald Press: Scottsdale, PA, 2000, 25th ed.). I felt empowered by the idea that I could address world hunger right from the confines of my own kitchen every time I cooked.

Some changes required more effort, a testimony to my intractability. I balked at the "nuisance" of recycling. Once I actually began, however, it proved unexpectedly easy. I formed new habits in spite of myself. Now it seems natural to wash out used cans and bottles and drop them in the recyclable bin rather than the trash. I am gratified too whenever I take a step toward curb-

Thursday's child has far to go.

ing consumption. There is a bolstering jolt of reinforcement to my self-esteem every time I perform one of these simple acts.

Simplifying our lives can begin anywhere. It can begin by saying "no" to any invitation, no matter how attractive, if it is something you do not want to do. Choosing not to buy paper towels and using a rag to wipe up spills, taking an hour each week to play board games or walk to the park together—each of us begins the process in our own way.

The bad news is you have to do it yourself. The good news is doing it yourself means you have the freedom to simplify in your own way, at your own rate. A lot of little changes add up to big results.

Thank you, God, that we are unique and that you love us as we are. Give us the perspective to see our little lives as important because they— and we—matter to you. Amen.

Friday

Friday's child is loving and giving.

Hear Here

PROVERBS 9:1–6

When we first moved to Milwaukee, we noticed light poles at many intersections wrapped with red, white, and blue bands and bearing the letters "EZ." We wondered about the significance of these windings. I conjectured they were a promotion for a local radio station that featured "easy listening" and bore the call letters "WEZW." I was wrong. The following year I heard the city police chief report on the "'Easy Does It' Enforcement Zone" program. The police department missed its mark with me.

I recall a similar instance from childhood. Our city had a huge black ornate Victorian clock standing in the middle of a downtown block. It was the promotional totem of one city bank. Around the clock face were the words "TIME TO SAVE." Through my childhood those enigmatic words possessed inscrutable significance. I could not puzzle out the meaning. I tried various combinations and interpretations, but all efforts at decoding proved fruitless.

"TIME TO SAVE . . ." What? "TIME TO SAVE" . . . stamps? Did, perhaps, "TIME TO SAVE" mean we ought to save up all

Friday's child is loving and giving.

the little ticks and tocks and put them in a basket for future use? I altered the word order: "TO SAVE TIME." I had heard of time- and labor-saving devices. The big clock might be admonishing the populace to greater efficiency. I reworded the message in yet another way: "SAVE TIME TO . . ." I liked this variant very much. I got to fill in the blank. If I did some unpleasant chore quickly enough, I would "save time to" read or color. With all my permutations and reinterpretations, I never stumbled upon the correct one. From the bank's perspective it was obvious the slogan meant "TIME TO SAVE your money in an account with them."

We seem so often to be talking mostly to ourselves. We know what we mean. We send out our messages but fail to adequately consider our audience. Folks are eager to talk and tell, but often we'd be better advised to listen.

David and I have turned one kind of self-talk into a game. When we are driving and notice a vanity license plate, we compete for the most outlandish possible interpretation. What do you make of "D9OMYT" or "LVDSNY" or "MSOVA"? Recently we found a particularly provocative plate, "PD 4 PD." Our best efforts include "Parental Discretion for Patagonian Dances" and "Public Dismay for Pagan Deities." As our game suggests, vanity license plate holders are talking mostly to themselves.

Our executive minister tells the story of visiting a small rural congregation one Sunday morning. He parked his car and walked to the front entrance of the church. The doors were locked. He knocked, but no one answered. Thinking he had gotten the time wrong, he returned to his car to check his notes. As he sat, he saw a car enter a driveway in front of him and proceed toward the rear of the building. The executive minister followed and found

Friday's child is loving and giving.

a parking lot and rear entrance he hadn't known was there. Other cars arrived. Everyone bustled through the back door.

The executive told the congregation of his experience at their front door. "Oh yes," came the reply, "we always keep those doors locked. We only ever use the back door."

Smiling ruefully, the executive minister responded, "But what if someone comes who doesn't know you use the back door? They might conclude you weren't having services."

Before we tell our story we need to listen. As the adage goes, "We have one mouth and two ears so that we will listen twice as much as talk." Without closing the loop, the police department never knew if its "EZ" emphasis was communicating. My hometown bank assumed that its slogan was self-evident. The holders of vanity plates believe they are making an intelligible statement. The fact is, if we don't listen to the other, we don't know if we are being heard.

I'm a teacher; I like to impart information. I'm a pastor; I do a lot of talking. I'm a storyteller; I like to tell. Each of my roles is gratifying. None of them, however, compares with the experience of being listened to. One of the best gifts I ever received was when a friend returned to a subject I had glossed over, saying, "Yes, but how are you? I really want to know." And then he waited for the answer. He listened.

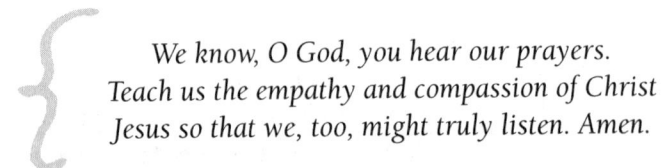

*We know, O God, you hear our prayers.
Teach us the empathy and compassion of Christ
Jesus so that we, too, might truly listen. Amen.*

Saturday's child works hard for a living. **Saturday**

(Don't) Do It Yourself

PSALM 139:1–12

I found—let's call him—"Larry" in the local shopper. The wind had pulled up a shingle at the front of our house, there was a slight leak in the enclosed front porch, and I don't climb out on roofs anymore.

It was apparent from our first conversation that Larry was as much interested in making a relationship as in mending roofs. A tall, shambling man in his mid-forties, Larry told how he was alone now. His wife had left, his kids were grown and gone, and something was wrong with his heart. The doctors were trying to find out what.

I had long ago discovered that power tools and I were not friends, and I had also learned that dealing with handymen is not the same as employing "bonded, certified contractors who are recommended by the local association of home remodelers." Larry, like most handymen, needs to talk. He also needs to be closely supervised. Most practically, he needs not to be completely paid until the job has been done to satisfaction.

After he repaired the roof, I invited Larry to our house again, this time to give me a new ceiling in my office and to paint the

Saturday's child works hard for a living.

kitchen. He brought along with him—let's say—"Curly." Shortly on Curly's footsteps came "Moe."

The three of them are upstairs now. It is the third—last, I pray—day of the job. You would not believe the number of holes in the wall necessary to run a new circuit for a proposed air-conditioner. I have counted five so far, not including the little hole they made in the stairway ceiling carrying up the drywall.

You would not believe the dust these three musketeers make, the number of times I must remind them to close the door (or go shut it myself because they have not heard me), and the mess they leave at the end of the day.

Moe is the electrician of the crew. He has told me many times, "I'm going to give you a new box there at the light fixture; I don't like the look of the old one." He has repeatedly inquired, "You sure you don't want your sockets up higher?" Every time we have had this exchange, he has told me, "That's where I always put them in my house." Then, each time, he reassures me, "I put the grounding screw in for you. Now you don't have anything to worry about."

With any of the three, it's not so much what they say, as why. Loneliness, I think. Moe, like his two colleagues, spends at least as much time talking as working. The three often go away to get a supply they have forgotten, and when they break for lunch, they are gone for at least two hours.

So why with all this mess and disruption and bother do I employ these guys? Three reasons. One is money. If I hired top-of-the-line contractors, this job would cost nearly twice as much. Another reason is that these guys care. Curly spent eight hours—eight uncompensated hours—recreating the arch in the ceiling upstairs. He expended so much energy and effort not because the

Saturday's child works hard for a living.

arch was necessary and not because I demanded it but simply because he wanted the challenge and joy of making something beautiful.

My deepest reason for employing the Three Musketeers, however, comes from the implicit connection we have with each other. Like me, they are living nearer to the margins than to the mainstream. Like me, they are making a serious attempt to combine work and play. They have fallen to the bottom—perhaps out of—the middle class, they wear their hearts on their sleeves and have little restraint or pretension, and they are vulnerable, both emotionally and economically.

Hiring them reminds me of what really matters. The "how" of work is at least as important as the "what," but the most important of all is the "who." Larry, Curly, and Moe are men who work for me, to be sure, but they are first and foremost human beings, made, like me, in the image of God. They are my brothers.

Our house was built in the early 1920s. There is much that needs to be done here, and I am sure the Three Musketeers will return. When they do, the job all finished and the money all paid, I'll show them these words. I think they'll be very interested to be included in a book, and then undoubtedly we'll talk about it.

Thank you for work, Lord God, and thank you for workers. Give us all meaningful work to do and the grace to move our work in the direction of fun.
Amen.

Sunday

*But the child born on the Sabbath day
is bright and blithe and bonny and gay.*

Close-up

1 CORINTHIANS 13:11–12

Chuck Close is a contemporary portrait artist. Early in his career the art world recognized his talent for photographic realism. His work is unmistakable and impossible to miss. Close paints colossal canvases of the faces of his friends. Some of his canvases take a year or more to complete. His paintings are acts of love; the intimacy of the relationship parallels the intimacy he experiences working on the portrait. In his close-up paintings, he reproduces every blot, wrinkle, and blemish. Each painting is a meditation on that person's life story. People are jarred as they view Close's work. His paintings tell the truth about who the particular subject is and in so doing tell us something about who we are.

When Chuck Close was a boy, his teachers dismissed him as stupid. He was awkward and uncoordinated. His mind just didn't work like other children's. Only in doing art did he excel. While other kids dreamed of becoming firefighters, Chuck Close was dreaming of being an artist. Since he wasn't skilled in games and sports, he needed a way to attract and keep friends. He cajoled

But the child born on the Sabbath day is bright and blithe and bonny and gay.

his father into building him a puppet stage. Chuck designed the puppets and performed the plays, so he became a center of neighborhood activity.

When he graduated from high school, Close's transcript was so deficient he was admitted only to the nearby community college (because they had to take him). His art studies began and eventually led him to Yale. From there he was launched into a meteorically successful career. Chuck Close's triumph testifies to the indomitability of the human spirit. His life reminds us that we are differently abled and differently disabled. The challenge is to find what we do well and pursue it.

We all have limitations. Some of mine are external and obvious. I am extremely myopic. If I put my glasses in an unusual place, I must ask David to come and find them for me. Some of my disabilities don't show outwardly. No one knows, just by looking, that I am dyslexic or that I come from a dysfunctional family. Chuck Close reminds us that what's wrong with us does not matter. What does matter is rightly using our gifts. Chuck Close was, by all usual standards, a "failure" who became a phenomenal success.

From Yale, Close burst upon the art scene and received great appreciation and acclaim. Even so, he has never stopped growing. His continuing growth is due to his outlook on life. His philosophy can be summed up like this: "Some people think the point is solving problems; others believe the point is posing new ones."

At the pinnacle of his success, in the late 1980s, life posed a new problem for Close. An artery in his spine burst, leaving him a quadriplegic. Experts from both the medical and artistic worlds declared his career over. Chuck Close didn't listen. He spent

But the child born on the Sabbath day is bright and blithe and bonny and gay.

months in rehabilitation until he was able to stand and even take a few steps. He regained partial use of his arms and hands and resumed painting. Although he must still use a wheelchair and strap the brush to his hand, Close continues to live out his passion for portraiture.

Viewed from one angle, Chuck Close's story is a tragic tale of serial misfortune. From the opposite angle, however, his is a story of heroic victory. It is a model of the Christian story: out of death comes new life. Chuck Close points us toward hope— hope for overcoming disability, hope for surmounting adversity, hope when all seems hopeless. Chuck Close paints with his life and brushes a close-up picture of the power of human spirit.

> *Thank you, dear God, for the example of courageous Chuck Close. Pose us challenges that enable us to overcome our disabilities. Transform us that we might reflect the Easter story. Amen.*

But the child born on the Sabbath day is bright and blithe and bonny and gay.

Where You Can View Chuck Close's Work
Akron Art Institute, Ohio
Carnegie Institute, Pittsburgh, Pennsylvania
Des Moines Art Center, Iowa
Georgia Museum of Art, University of Georgia, Athens
The High Museum of Art, Atlanta, Georgia
Madison Art Museum, Wisconsin
Milwaukee Art Museum, Wisconsin
Minneapolis Institute of Art, Minnesota
Museum of Art, Fort Lauderdale, Florida
Museum of Contemporary Art, Chicago, Illinois
Museum of Fine Arts, Boston, Massachusetts
National Gallery of Art, Washington, D.C.
National Gallery of Canada, Ottawa
Philadelphia Museum of Art, Pennsylvania
St. Louis Art Museum, Missouri
Seattle Art Museum, Washington
Toledo Museum, Ohio
Virginia Museum of Fine Arts, Richmond
Walker Art Center, Minneapolis, Minnesota
Whitney Museum of American Art, New York, New York
Yale University Art Gallery, New Haven, Connecticut

Monday

Monday's child is fair of face.

The Chameleon Factor

1 Samuel 20:35–42

Are you at least a little bit lonely? If your social calendar is full and you have more friends than you know what to do with, please skip this conversation, but if you'd like more people in your life, including some new close friends, here is the secret recipe for making human relationship.

The Twelve-Steppers are on to something. They urge their members to attend meetings regularly and frequently. Their point is that we human beings resemble chameleons. Both persons and lizards fit in wherever they are. We pick the folks we want to be with, and they call forth from us the qualities that will help us belong to their society.

Fitting in doesn't always seem easy, but it really is. It has just three parts. First, be there. Go where folks you want to meet are. Second, be there a lot. Don't just drop in occasionally; become a regular. Third, choose to be with folks you want to be with. After all, in order to care about each other, we need first to know each other, but we can't know one another until we meet.

Monday's child is fair of face.

Think about it. Where do most husbands and wives meet? Work, school, or church—some location they inhabit both frequently and regularly. It's true not only for husbands and wives but also for everyone else.

So let's get practical. If you want more people in your life, you must go where they are. Where is that? Well, it depends. It depends upon what you care about.

If you like to drink beer and play volleyball, hop in the car at about six in the evening and go looking for a bar that has a volleyball court next to it. If work is the most important thing in your life, find the work group that has people who share your values. It may be a union, a professional association, or something like a softball league or Toastmasters chapter. It depends upon the kind of work you do and the level you have achieved.

Another place you might look, especially if you live in a city, is your neighborhood. Folks are already near; you need only slow down and say hello more often. Block clubs exist, after all, just as much for social reasons as for neighborhood safety.

Survey your interests and values, and then be willing to experiment. Do you care about ethics, morality, and spirituality? You'll find like-minded friends in nearby churches. Do you like politics? Especially at campaign time, candidates clamor for whatever help they can get. In off-campaign times, the really dedicated gather to strategize future campaigns.

Ethnic identity, hobbies, intellectual interests, genealogy, even favorite kinds and vintages of automobiles—the things people care about are very different. The good news is that your group is waiting. All you have to do is find out where.

Monday's child is fair of face.

> *Thank you that we can discover how to connect better and make new friends. Thank you that in the mystery of human connection there are a few basic principles that all of us can learn. Amen.*

Tuesday's child is full of grace.

Tuesday

Diary Entry

PSALM 1:1 – 3

12/11—Discovered I lost my wallet last night. I can hear all the voices in my head saying, "Good Heavens! You'd lose you head if it wasn't fastened on." "Tsk, tsk, tsk. Irresponsible—again." I feel terrible. Now all the credit cards and driver's license will need to be replaced. One good thing: I had all my Christmas shopping done. I won't need to worry about not having credit cards. Sadly, all my Christmas cash was also in the wallet. Probably a lost cause, but I'll call the store to see if anyone turned it in.

12/12—No good. *Lucy Locket lost her pocket. Kitty Fisher found it.* I wish someone would find my wallet. Called store. Nothing matching its description had been turned in. I can't be too upset. I was able to buy everyone's gifts—except D's. I suspect it fell out of my purse in the parking lot. I *know* I had it at the bookstore, and then I used a credit card at the last store. It had to have happened there. Is it possible that someone took it out of my purse while I was loading the car?

12/14—Got new license today. Big mixup. DMV had already

Tuesday's child is full of grace.

sent me home once because I didn't have adequate proof of identity. Brought D back hoping he would admit to knowing me. Nice young football-player type got tired of waiting but gave us his number before he left. We moved up eight places! Still more than an hour wait. The form says one's spouse can vouch for you if s/he has own license. Nevertheless, they almost sent us away again. Fortunately, another clerk overheard conversation and intervened. Am seeing the ways one person's error (sin) affects others. In this case specifically D, since he had to wait with me. Even so, he still admitted to knowing me. What a sweetheart!

12/17—We were talking about the wallet yesterday. Have concluded that at this point not much chance of ever seeing it again. With the economy so stinky, whoever found the wallet has probably already spent the money. We canceled the credit cards so there's no chance of getting a surprise bill for a home entertainment center or a Lexus or—who knows?

Jane scared me with story of friend who has been dealing with identity theft. Said that once they get your SS# they have access to all kinds of info. Did I have my SS card in wallet? Of course. Do I feel like a fool? Of course. Can only hope whoever found wallet is too stupid to figure out how to steal my identity.

12/20—Going to Toni and Ken's. If conversation flags, can tell wallet story. Looked at picture on license. Made me realize how short life is. Have known Toni forever. Want to tell them how important they have been to me. Relationships so much more important than $$.

12/24—Can you believe it? The store called. They have my wallet—after all this time! Never expected to see it again. I'll go pick it up later this morning. Nothing of value in it now. Credit

Tuesday's child is full of grace.

cards have been canceled, license no longer current. Always liked that wallet. I'll be glad to have it back.

A Christmas miracle. Who'd a thought? The wallet was turned in with everything, *everything* in tact—credit cards, SS card, driver's license, and *money*! I can hardly believe it. There are honest people in the world, even in hard times. Take that, Ebenezer Scrooge!

> *Thank you, God, for all the surprises. Open our eyes to the wonder around us. Open our hearts to the goodness of others. Keep us from becoming cynical and suspicious without cause. Grant us the innocence of Christmas all year through. Amen.*

Wednesday

Wednesday's child is full of woe.

Free Lunch

Exodus 16:9–12

When I was in first grade, I got my first lunchbox. It was decorated in floral designs and had a pink plastic handle. Inside was a small Thermos. On my first day of ownership, I was so excited I had my mother pack my lunchbox so I could eat from it sitting on our front porch.

One day while waiting for the school bus, I put my lunchbox down in order to play jump rope. The bus came and I got on, but my lunchbox didn't. Lunchtime arrived and in a sudden flash of horrible realization, I knew I had neither lunchbox nor lunch. I was mortified. I was sure I was in big trouble. I didn't know the magnitude of the sin I committed. I knew only that I was a sinner. I told no one. I felt heartsick. It was only a small stretch to physical illness. I felt terrible. I put my head down on my desk. When the teacher asked, I could truthfully reply, "I don't feel well."

History repeats itself. Twenty-five years after I lost that lunchbox, I was on staff at a large historic church. My portfolio included serving as youth group counselor. The high school

Wednesday's child is full of woe.

Sunday school class was painting the gym. The mother of one of the boys in the class proposed sending out for burgers. While the orders were being taken, I made myself scarce. I didn't have enough money to pay for soda, let alone lunch. Lunch arrived and while the others ate, I went on an unnecessary errand to the storeroom.

When I judged the coast was clear, I returned to work. "Where were you?" Charlie's mom asked. "You weren't around when we were taking orders so I just got you a burger and fries."

"Oh," I smiled weakly. "I had to . . . check some supplies. Thanks, but I'm not really hungry. Maybe one of the guys will want seconds."

After everyone else had gone home, I was left alone with the final details of cleaning up.

As I was crumpling newspaper into a plastic garbage sack, I found the burger—whole and uneaten—still in its wrapper. The french fries had deteriorated to a state of greasy, wilted limpness. I left them where they lay; but the sandwich I rescued.

I was ravenous by this time, but I was also in the throes of humiliation. I weighed the implications along with the heft of the package in my palm. Here was the sandwich. Here was I, hungry and alone. Nobody need ever know. I ripped off the wrapping and bolted the burger.

Jesus says, "Blessed are you who hunger now, for you will be satisfied" (Luke 6:21) and "Blessed are those who hunger and thirst for righteousness" (Matthew 5:6). I managed the hunger, but the righteousness escaped me. Jesus says we are to recognize and accept our dependence upon God's mercy and goodness. We can't fully accept God's love unless we can accept love from other human beings.

Wednesday's child is full of woe.

The lunchroom ladies at Fall-Meyer Elementary School would have been glad to provide lunch for a little girl who had forgotten her lunchbox. Charlie's mom too was eager for the chance to be hospitable and gracious. Part of righteousness is living our authentic selves, with or without our lunchboxes. Sometimes we are givers, sometimes receivers. Our only real danger lies in being exclusively one or the other. I had swallowed a story of being beholden to no one, but I couldn't (wouldn't) swallow my pride and admit that I needed someone else's help. Such small need, such big denial.

> *God of all good and perfect gifts, teach us to ask so that we can receive what you offer. Open our spirits and lives to your goodness. Send your Spirit into our hearts to teach us the words "yes" and "thank you." Amen.*

Thursday's child has far to go.   **Thursday**

Death of the Dining Room

1 CORINTHIANS 8:7–13

Once upon a time, almost every home—even the most modest of them—had a place called "the dining room." It was actually a room all to itself, separate from the kitchen, living room, and every other space. A most curious activity took place in this location. They called that activity "dining."

Dining and eating were not quite the same thing. True enough, dining did involve eating, but there were an additional host of activities that came along. When one dined, for example, one also talked, and listened. Furthermore, the talking was of a certain kind. This kind of talk was called "social conversation." The topics of social conversation ranged from the minutia of the speakers' routines to deep discussions of great ideas. Absolutely prohibited were such forms of discourse as lecturing, nagging, and yelling (although a generous measure of harmless gossip was often permitted).

The furnishings of the dining room varied in accordance with the taste and financial condition of the family. The main

Thursday's child has far to go.

piece of furniture in the dining room was the table, followed closely by six, eight, ten, or more chairs, which were placed around the table. The diners sat on those chairs the whole meal long and ate the food that was served at the dining room table.

Other furniture in the dining room included a buffet and a server. The buffet was a kind of specialized cupboard that contained the family's china and crystal. China is . . .

Well, never mind. Dining rooms have gone by the wayside now, as have china and crystal, and we who survive are poorer for the loss. Instead of dining rooms, we now have "family rooms," where the family hardly ever gathers, and "great rooms," which are used for entertaining our guests with canapés and cocktails. With the passing of the dining room we have sacrificed an important expression of connection. Families once gathered in their dining rooms to celebrate holidays and important milestones. Often three or four generations sat down together, including unmarried aunts and uncles and even a distant cousin or two.

Fine dining is expensive in terms of both money and time. The contents of the dining room, especially the plate, crystal, and dinner service, once represented a significant portion of the family's wealth. Moreover, it takes a good deal longer to prepare for and clean up after dining than it does either to pour some cereal into a bowl or run out to McDonalds.

We have two aunts, both now in their eighties, who still use their dining room. They no longer serve every meal there, but they do serve at least one each day. We use our own dining room much less often, but still occasionally. If you are fortunate enough to know someone who has, and uses, their dining room, try to wangle an invitation to dine. It's the only way—the actual

Thursday's child has far to go.

experience of the event—to discover why there are still some folks left who think it worth the energy and time.

The "good silver," the fine china, the polished wood surface of the dining room table (dining room tables are always made of wood, never of plastic or some other manufactured product), leisurely eating, social conversation, and real cloth napkins—an investment capable of returning a rich reward.

You are invited to our house Sunday after worship, and we promise to use the good china. Be prepared to linger over a leisurely meal and engage in social conversation.

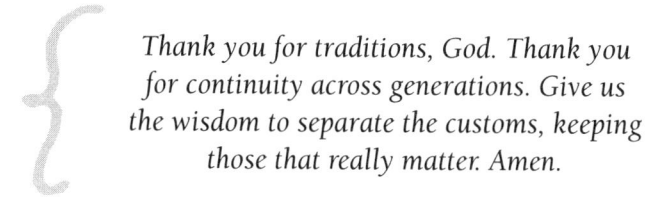

> *Thank you for traditions, God. Thank you for continuity across generations. Give us the wisdom to separate the customs, keeping those that really matter. Amen.*

Friday

Friday's child is loving and giving.

Can Community Be Virtual?

EPHESIANS 2:11–18

Let's call her Lucy.

Now in her mid-fifties, Lucy is becoming increasingly isolated. She has many fears, many anxieties, and more than a few regrets. She also has a new computer.

"I'm on the Net," she says. "My cyber-relationships are very important. Just the other day I had a long talk with a seventeen-year-old. He asked me all sorts of questions he never could have in person. How neat computers are. I really think I did him some good."

Perhaps so, but Lucy reminds me of a professor I had in graduate school. He was a great fan of "distance learning." "Just think of it," he said. "No student need ever be isolated again. Even in the most rural areas, all they must do is turn on their computers. They are immediately connected, part of the virtual community."

He was right. They are connected but only most superficially. The learners can see and hear each other but neither smell nor touch one another. True communication is much more than mere seeing and hearing.

Friday's child is loving and giving.

For example, the other day Donald and I went to the Milwaukee River Parkway just to talk. We found a comfortable spot beneath some trees and flopped down. To our right, the falls gushed. To our left a man fished. Down the river, swollen with recent rain, floated a mother duck with eight ducklings in tow.

Donald and I were talking about all those deep things twenty-four-year-old men talk about with older male friends. In an hour by the riverside we covered Christianity, Buddhism, the meaning of family, and most of the differences between the United States and Brazil, among other things. As I say, it was a very wide-ranging conversation!

In that hour many things happened that would not be perceived in a "distance learning event." A new family of fishers replaced the man who was first there; we greeted each other and discussed the prospects. Two Glendale police cars sped by, prompting Donald and me to share our experiences of the police. The swollen river rushed, the little duck family couldn't make its turn, and the ducklings were swept over the falls. The mother rose in a frantic explosion of wings and went down to see what she could retrieve. All these things and who knows how many more were part of Donald's and my conversation.

In his day, Jesus' opponents were advocates of "virtual" faith. They wanted the appearance of faithfulness. They wanted to fulfill their religious obligations but without religion making deep demands on them. They made a show of their piety—fasting with long faces, writing big checks for the temple offering plate, dispensing alms when they had an audience.

I think Jesus would have equal difficulty with virtual faith and virtual community. It is a community of appearances, almost but not quite the real thing. Computer connection buffers and

Friday's child is loving and giving.

protects us. We don't even have to use our real names. We can weave webs of illusion around ourselves to ensnare others into relationship with our totally manufactured self. It is an abstraction of real relationship. We are settling for a piece of the whole reality. It denies the importance of the Incarnation. Although Jesus could and did do "distance healing," he more often mingled with misfits, allowed the unclean to touch him, socialized with outcasts. The message of Incarnation is that God in Jesus made himself vulnerable to us.

It's too easy, too convenient, with a computer to turn away, not see the pain in a face, smell the metallic odor of fear, hear the edge of challenge in a voice. Relationship becomes like watching TV. When I want entertainment I can logon; when I've gotten my fix I can logoff. There is none of the ambiguous messiness of actual engagement.

I think of Lucy at her computer. Sitting alone in her air-conditioned upstairs, she pretends that the words flowing back and forth on her screen are evidence of genuine human connection. But they are not. They are mere shadows of the real thing.

I will not add to Lucy's isolation by emailing her these reflections on virtual and actual community. Instead, I'm going to knock on her door, take her hand, look her in the eye, sit across from her at the kitchen table, and make real human connection.

Thank you for fitting us together, God. Thank you for insisting that we are one people made for belonging with you. Teach us how to bridge the distances of barren isolation. Amen

Saturday's child works hard for a living.   **Saturday**

Microwaiver

ECCLESIASTES 2:4 – 11

We still don't have a microwave, and Lo-Ann's eighty-seven-year-old mother has managed to live quite successfully without a microwave her whole life long.

My mother does have a microwave, and she says, "For a long time all I used it for was heating up my coffee, but it's really easy to use, so I started buying those—what do you call them, 'microwavable meals'?"

"They're not bad," Mom says. Faint praise indeed from a woman who, like many in her generation, prides herself on her cooking.

"I don't cook much anymore," Mom says. "It's hard when you're alone. It seems hardly worth the energy."

Ah, but when she is not alone, Mom has no use whatsoever for her microwave. When the bridge group meets for dinner over at the clubhouse, Mom's pot roast or spaghetti or coconut cream pie is the talk of the evening.

Saturday's child works hard for a living.

"Of course, the microwave is worthless for those times," Mom says. "It wouldn't do at all, not when you want real food."

Microwaves seem inexpensive. A small one costs as little as sixty dollars, but the small ones are useful only for heating coffee and, of course, for cooking all those "what do you call them." Like all prepackaged, overly processed food, microwavable meals are very expensive. It is all quite seductive. First comes the tool, then the using. Now that I have a microwave, I buy popcorn and pizza puffs and stuffed jalapeño peppers just because I have a microwave to "cook" them in.

By the way, if you ever hear anyone extolling the low energy costs of microwaves, run like crazy. Of course, a given meal in a microwave consumes less energy than does conventional cooking, but it takes an awful lot of microwaving to make up for the initial cost, and then there are all those times when one uses the microwave just to heat up the coffee.

The sound of a microwave addict is heard in the land. "But all the benefits!" the voice cries. "Think of the convenience!"

It is true that microwaves are attractive to people who are in a tremendous hurry and must squeeze eating into their busy schedules. But wait! Is it good for us to be so busy that we must "squeeze in" eating? What kind of life is it that is so crammed with activity that meals are looked upon mostly as an interruption?

("But I am busy," you cry. "I need to save time." Please quit reading right this minute. You haven't a moment to lose! Turn to the story called "The Death of the Dining Room," and read it as fast as you can, before the next "must-do" arrives in your frantic schedule.)

Saturday's child works hard for a living.

The cost of the microwave is not only in coin. It is an aid to isolation, an encourager of living on the run, and an excuse for drinking stale coffee.

We suggested to Mom that she throw her microwave away. She thought about it for a moment but then looked up wistfully. "I would if I could," she said, "but I got used to it."

> *Thank You, God, for all the marvelous tools that make life easier. Give us clarity and wisdom, so we can choose the right tools and not let our things have mastery over our lives. Remind us of life's simple pleasures—a home-cooked meal ... a cup of fresh-brewed coffee. Amen.*

Sunday

*But the child born on the Sabbath day
is bright and blithe and bonny and gay.*

The Varieties of Prayer

1 THESSALONIANS 5:16–18

We often think of prayer as duty. What if prayer is privilege too?

We ordinarily think of prayer as our needing to talk. What if an equally important part is listening? Prayer is commonly associated mostly with words. What if the experience is expanded, and prayer includes any and all communication with God?

Making a few changes in our prayer life can bring us into fuller possession of the riches of God's blessing, so start each day with prayer. Make it a habit as inevitable as taking a shower or brushing your teeth. Go to a specific place at a designated time. Don't worry too much about what happens, and don't think too much about how you are feeling. Just do it—say for two weeks—and see what difference it makes.

Think of prayer not as duty but as privilege. Don't pray because you must but because you may. Come to prayer not from guilt and obligation but with hope and expectation. Think of yourself as a child coming to a parent who loves you very much indeed.

But the child born on the Sabbath day is bright and blithe and bonny and gay.

Instead of talking, listen. Oh, of course you can talk if you want to, that is, if you have anything to say. But don't stop praying when you run out of words. Stay and listen, believing that God wants to communicate with you even more than you want to communicate with God. The voice of God can be quite subtle. It is unlikely that you will hear sound you could tape record, so listen with the ears of faith and look with Jesus' eyes.

After you have followed these suggestions for two weeks, re-decide. Write down the process of your re-decision. What worked for you and what didn't? When you use the word "worked" with regard to prayer, what do you mean? Did you learn anything from this new way of praying and thinking about prayer?

Now ask yourself one final question. Why are you doing all this alone? Don't you know anyone else who prays? Are you so isolated that there is not another human being who would be overjoyed to share with you the adventure of growing closer to God?

Pastor, spouse, parent, friend, offspring—surely there is someone you care about and who cares about you with whom you can share. You might want to pray together. Failing that possibility, you might at least want to share each other's wisdom.

Making all of life a prayer is the surest way to find the joy in each and every moment. As we open ourselves more completely to God, we find ourselves more completely filled with joy and also with the other fruits of the Spirit: love, peace, kindness, gentleness, patience, goodness, faithfulness, and self-control.

We have a friend—let's call him Jason—who made the sorts of changes in his prayer life that we have been talking about here. After only two months of praying in new ways, he came to us

But the child born on the Sabbath day is bright and blithe and bonny and gay.

just as excited as he could be. "It works!" Jason said. "It really works. I used to think of prayer as hands folded, eyes closed, and maybe kneeling. Now I know I can pray anywhere. Do you know what? Even this conversation we are having right now—even this very conversation—could be prayer!"

> *Thank you that you love us where we are and as we are. Thank you that there is no earning or deserving when it comes to relationship with you. Teach us to believe it, and then to share. Amen.*

Monday's child is fair of face.

Monday

Mauled

2 CORINTHIANS 2:14 – 17

I went shopping at Brookview Mall the other day. I had a gift certificate for a store I only vaguely knew. It was an astonishing experience. Even more unsettling was the awareness that I was alone in my astonishment.

The store specializes in soaps, bath products, and aromatherapy. I watched teenage girls snatching products from the shelves and rushing to the cash register. I overheard two senior citizens debating the merits of various scents without mentioning the price. Was it only me? Hadn't anyone else noticed that the equivalent of most of these products could be purchased at the drugstore for a fraction of the cost? I spent my certificate and left the store shaking my head. I wanted to understand what was happening, but I was, initially, simply too stunned to think it through.

I was witnessing recreational shopping. People are lured to the prestige of the mall and become accustomed to its prices. They do not think to compare the products offered at the mall with others offered elsewhere. It becomes a shopping tautology:

Monday's child is fair of face.

If I buy my body lotion at the Bubble Bath Shop, the Bubble Bath Shop is where I look for body lotion. I am oblivious to other options. Since the drugstore and the discount retailer do not carry the Bubble Bath brand body lotion, there is no point in looking for the product there, so everyone goes to the mall.

Malls want their concourses filled with eager shoppers. The management sponsors promotions that draw crowds. There is reinforcement in the crush of people, all enjoying themselves as each hustles away in a different direction. The mall is a place to see and be seen. Here are attractive, expensively dressed people. As I move among them, I too feel more attractive and desirable. I must be, mustn't I? I must be one of them, for here I am among them. To be one of them I must look like them and behave as they do. They are shopping and buying. I too should shop and buy. All these people can't be wrong. This mall is the place to be!

Some reflection on the fate of another mall in town confirmed my analysis. Unlike Brookview, Highbridge failed. Before it closed I walked its nearly deserted hallways. The few other shoppers flitted like silent shadows. The mall had been driven to ruin by rumor. "Don't go there. Thugs hide under the cars in the parking lot and then jump out to slash you." "Don't go there. The gangs pick shoppers and cut them out of the crowd like wolves with sheep. They surround you and you can't escape." "Don't go there. They'll rear-end you. When you get out to check the damage, they'll carjack you."

People began avoiding Highbridge. The bigger, tonier stores couldn't justify keeping their doors open when there were so few customers. They moved to other, more profitable markets. With fewer stores, fewer people were attracted. The scent of failure was in the air. Highbridge was doomed. The proprietors have put

Monday's child is fair of face.

the property on the market. They hope to recover a few cents on each dollar of their investment.

Despite our apparent social sophistication, we are basically tribal creatures. We define ourselves by the company we seek and keep. We want to associate with sweet-smelling success and avoid failure's acrid stench. If we are judged by the company we keep, whom will I choose? Will it be the beautiful people who glide sleekly through the mall or the unloved and unlovely who flocked to Jesus?

Free us, loving God, to be our true selves. Enable us to define who we are as followers of Jesus, not the crowd. Rescue us from the temptation of "going along." We pray the mercy to look upon the hearts of others as you have done with us. Amen.

Tuesday

Tuesday's child is full of grace.

Walking in (Holy) Circles

PSALM 23

During Lent of 2002, for the first time, we walked a labyrinth. I was surprised by how deeply the experience touched my spirit. On the basis of that single walking I have many more questions than answers, but I think I learned some things worth sharing.

Physically, a labyrinth is like a maze but with one important difference. A maze has blind alleys and is a kind of puzzle to be solved. In a labyrinth there is only one way to walk, and the way in is the way out. There is a variety of forms of labyrinths. The one we walked is a copy of the most well-known labyrinth, that found in the Cathedral of Notre Dame de Chartres. There was a cross at the edge of our labyrinth, directly opposite the entrance.

The little pamphlet we were given before beginning suggests a number of ways of walking and a number of different strategies for maximizing the spiritual depth of the experience, but I suspect each person's walk will fit the individual walking, and I also imagine that there are a number of valid ways any single individual could walk.

Tuesday's child is full of grace.

The canvas circle spread on the floor seemed very unimpressive, hardly capable of providing a profound spiritual experience. The diameter of the circle is perhaps thirty feet, and the pathways of the labyrinth are hardly wide enough for one. These were the sorts of words going through my head as I entered the room, but then I remembered that I was in the presence of a spiritual tool thousands of years old. Perhaps I would do better to hope and trust. So I breathed deeply and allowed God's Sprit to empty me of suspicion and negativity. The invitation was to be quiet and calm and trusting. I was not the originator of blessing. I did not know what was "supposed" to happen, but God knew. God was both able and trustworthy. And so I began to walk.

A class of third-graders was walking the labyrinth when I entered. They were skipping quite gaily, but they were solemn too. There was something very serious in what they were doing, and some of them knew it.

The pamphlet says that the journey takes between twenty minutes to an hour or more. About five minutes into the walk, I was a bit confused, moving back and forth, and nothing was clear. Nevertheless, there was a kind of exhilaration within me, and I felt very purposeful. The children had finished. They were gathered along a wall putting on their shoes.

With my eyes closed, I stopped near the children to pray. They hushed each other at the urging of their teacher who seemed to want me to have a prayerful experience, and I sensed my deep connection to these children and their teacher.

At the center, one is invited to pause, wait in expectation of a blessing, and remain until receiving a spiritual prompting to leave. I sensed it was time to go, began walking, and felt a deep panic. The way in is the way out, isn't it? Did I do it wrong? I

Tuesday's child is full of grace.

stood almost in tears until I realized: "wrong" had no meaning in this experience. There was only willing or not willing to be with God.

Especially on the journey out, I found myself passionately lured by the cross. Whenever I turned toward it, I stopped and prayed. Whenever I turned away, I knew myself to be a betrayer of Jesus.

It seemed that I had been walking a long time since the third graders left (I later discovered the entire experience consumed about forty-five minutes). Two young teens were with me then. They walked rapidly and were at least as interested in each other as in the experience, yet they too were surprisingly serious, even solemn.

Usually, walking in circles means that we are confused and frustrated. Walking the labyrinth, however, makes the circles more meaningful. The goal is ahead, and the goal is sure, but it is necessary to get there obliquely. Very much like life itself, I conclude. I have since learned that there is an outdoor labyrinth nearby. We are going to find it as soon as spring is surely here.

I think the forty-five minutes on canvas on a gym floor will stretch to two hours or more once we are out on the grass and underneath the trees.

Thank you, Lord, for the circles of life. Thank you that even when we do not know where we are going, you do, and that you are waiting for us to make it home to you. Amen.

Wednesday's child is full of woe. **Wednesday**

Heal Thyself

PSALM 128

"Cut through all the fluff," Dr. Richard A. Biek said, "and you'll find that modern medicine has made real advances on only four fronts: sanitation, nutrition, inoculation, and trauma repair." Biek was once health officer for the city of Milwaukee. It was some years ago when he said those words, and he might amend them slightly now but not, we suspect, a great deal. Dr. Biek's words have long held for us powerful and extensive implications.

The primary implication is that we are responsible for our own health. To the extent that we can benefit from the real good of modern medicine, we should, but if Dr. Biek is right, we will not spend much time doctoring.

Right on the heels of this primary implication—indeed, fighting for first place—is another. There is not a whole lot we can do about the state of our health. It is still true that the two factors that most influence how long we live are not much in our control. The first factor is our genetic inheritance, and no one can go back and choose new biological parents.

Wednesday's child is full of woe.

The second factor is accidents. Of course we can avoid those situations where accidents are more likely. We, for example, are on the road as little as possible on Friday and Saturday evenings when there are a lot of drunks driving. But accidents—the very word reminds us—are not under our control.

Now that we are aging, on those mornings when the arthritis kicks up, we often think of Dr. Biek's words. Sure, get in the hot shower as quickly as we can, and let it warm away the stiffness. But don't spend any more time than absolutely necessary thinking about the discomfort.

Because, you see, the inevitable fact is we are all going to die. As a pastor friend used to say after eating, "Well, one meal closer to the last." Some of his listeners were offended. Others were amused. We cast our vote for amusement.

As pastors, we have seen a bit more than our share of death and dying, so we are convinced of the truth that the best way to prepare for a good death is to live well. Wear your seatbelts, quit smoking (if you ever started), get some exercise without being obsessive about it, and pay attention to what your body is telling you. But pass the sour cream, please, so I can put some on this baked potato. I've counted the cost, and I'm willing to risk some elevated cholesterol. On the other hand, do not pass the bourbon. I've counted the cost and decided that life is so short and sweet that I do not want to pass through it drugged.

To a large extent, we are responsible for our health. If we try to pass that responsibility off to another, we succeed only in deluding ourselves. Modern medicine can sometimes accomplish amazing things, but it is more like a bandage than a cure-all for everything that ails us.

Wednesday's child is full of woe.

Thank you for the gift of health, dear God, and thank you for the illnesses and infirmities that remind us our time is limited and how we spend it is in large measure up to us. Amen.

Thursday

Thursday's child has far to go.

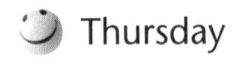

Penny Wise and Pound...

Luke 14:28–30

Some friends of ours recently bought a new car. They went all out. Upscaled a level or two above the perfectly good car they had traded in and added some bells and whistles. Having made that $38,000 purchase, our friends did a very interesting thing. They decided they needed to restrict their driving because they weren't sure they could afford the gasoline, and, after all, you wouldn't want to prematurely wear out a $38,000 car.

"Penny wise and pound foolish," Ben Franklin said. Our friends' new-car-driving policy reminds us not only of Benjamin Franklin but also of Ray's advice for building wealth.

Ray had inherited some money, but most of his wealth came through marriage. His wife's parents were farmers in the near suburbs at just the right time. Piece by piece, they sold off their acreage and purchased houses and apartments in the city. Ray's wife was their only child. So Ray didn't have any particular need to watch his pennies, and mostly he didn't. He owned an airplane, for example, which he flew around the Midwest basically for fun.

Thursday's child has far to go.

For some reason, though, Ray was very concerned about our financial well-being. His conversations with us often took a money-managing turn. The advice that we have treasured most fondly over the years is his suggestion about our frequent trips to and through Chicago.

"You know that little stretch of the Illinois Toll Road," Ray said, "before it joins up with the Kennedy. You can avoid the toll road completely. U.S. 41 goes straight through, and there are only eight or so stoplights. In fact, if you go down 41, you'll even save on gas because it's a straight shot. The time will work out about the same, though, because of those traffic signals. Take my advice and avoid the toll road. Your savings will really add up."

The savings that Ray was urging consist of $1.25 each way. We never did bother to calculate the miles, therefore gas savings that Ray's "straight shot" would provide us because the truth is we prefer the safety and convenience of the toll road.

Ray and our car-buying friends, we think, have something in common. This talk of saving money, we believe, is meaningful in only a very symbolic way. One dollar and a quarter at a time, after all, is going to have to be very often repeated if it's going to result in anything like wealth. Similarly, one would have to not drive a good many miles to come up with a $38,000 savings.

On the other hand, let's see. Maybe we've missed something here. Let's do the numbers. Ten trips a year, at $2.50 a trip, comes to $25.00. In twenty years, assuming they never again raise the tolls, we would have $500, and then what? Find a good investment, perhaps, and wait another twenty years for it to appreciate. Maybe we should just count the cost right now, making sure we have exact change to toss into the hopper at the next toll plaza.

Thursday's child has far to go.

> *Thank you for the truth, dear God.*
> *Thank you that we do not need to pretend;*
> *that we are invited to live up front and*
> *be honest with others, ourselves, and you.*
> *Amen.*

Friday's child is loving and giving. **Friday**

Keep Connected with Kids

PSALM 92:12–15

Ours is an age-segregated society. We work toward integrating diversity into many aspects of our lives, but when it comes to age we often keep the generations apart. Businesses from clothing shops to restaurants to radio stations cater to particular age cohorts. You enter and know immediately the intended audience—the teen scene, Boomers, Gen-Xers, or "blue hairs." Even churches tend to attract particular age groups.

One of our elderly mothers lives in a senior citizens' complex. Her life has been virtually child-free for years. There is even a rule at her facility stating that minors are not allowed to sleep over more than two consecutive nights.

We feel more comfortable with those our own age. We share a group understanding. We've lived through the same periods of history, experienced similar cultural peaks and valleys, had the same economic struggles. It's easier to get on with folks like ourselves, but our lives are much poorer as a result.

Friday's child is loving and giving.

Often, relating with an adjacent generation is difficult. They are, after all, either our parents or our children. Skipping a generation, however, is a different story. Jumping generations makes communication happen.

Linking children and grandparents brings a host of mutual benefits. Kids get the attention they need and crave. Grandparents receive an infusion of child energy, enthusiasm, and excitement. Kids get a break from the rules and rigidities of their nuclear families and revel in being indulged by Gramma and Grampa. Grandparents have the pleasures of childcare without the burdens of permanent responsibility since the children soon go back to Mom and Dad. The parents themselves get an advantage from cultivating cross-generational contact. They get a break from being on duty 24–7.

There are many reasons generation jumping works so well. Grandparents have seen it all. They've already made the mistakes the children haven't even thought about yet. Grandparents have greater tolerance for their grandchildren since they weren't directly involved in forming their habits. Kids are more likely to listen to the different voice of a grandparent because the kids themselves feel listened to. They don't have to be so rebellious since it is obvious even to a quite little child that a grandparent has a wealth of experience that one does not have oneself. The young provide evidence of hope and possibility. They are reminders of spring days when the branch is leafy green. Youth is moldable, formable, impressionable. They remind us of both our power and our responsibility because youngsters are so tender, vulnerable, and dependent.

Age, on the other hand, teaches us about endurance and strength. Fruit comes only from a mature tree. Through the tales

Friday's child is loving and giving.

of our elders we learn who we are and where we have come from. We learn our family tree and discover our roots. Elders remind us of the inevitable cycles of which we are a part: We all grow old and die. Elders become more venerable as they become more vulnerable to life's ending.

But as the gap in our ages widens, we have less and less in common, so we are less and less likely to stay in connection. The other side of that coin is that people who are the most different from us are the very ones who can teach us the most. Cross-generational relationships are like a forest composed of trees in various stages of growth. The whiplike saplings are just beginning. The gnarled and broken oaks are near their end. All abiding together, they make the forest both beautiful and healthy.

> *Thank you for the stages of life. Help us connect with each other over the whole span of living so we can all play our part in the family of God. Amen.*

Saturday

Saturday's child works hard for a living.

Going Against the Flow

ISAIAH 40:1 – 8

It's confession time. Our confession is that on Sunday evening in the summer, while driving north on I–43 through downtown Milwaukee, we see that huge stream of traffic heading toward Chicago and are more self-congratulatory than is probably good for us. We are going against the flow. Do you remember those ducks on the Milwaukee River (see "Can Community Be Virtual?")? The baby ducks were trying to swim upstream but couldn't. Going against the flow was too difficult; they got swept over the falls.

It is hard to go against the flow. Sometimes it is even dangerous. One danger is defying the wisdom of the mainstream. Positions and practices humankind has chosen over the ages represent the collective wisdom of our species. Bucking the trend means living in tension with that wisdom. It is also dangerous to go with the flow of course. As the ducks learned, the current sometimes takes over, and one is swept over the falls.

Nevertheless, we celebrate the wonderful exuberance of going against the flow. Swimming upstream is fun, partly because

Saturday's child works hard for a living.

it is difficult. Think about salmon furiously climbing fish ladders as they fight upstream for the sake of creativity. For the salmon, the creativity is literal, the birth of a new generation of fish. For us human beings, the creativity is of a wondrous variety of kinds, but for both fish and people creativity means struggling against the current.

At eight o'clock on a sunny summer morning, the traffic flows east on Silver Spring Drive, headed for the expressway. We are not in that flow. Instead we sit on the bank. We sit on our patio having coffee and marveling at our rich contentment. Horns sound, tires squeal, and the river rushes on, but we have paddled our canoe to a quiet backwater and are relaxing in the sun.

In January, the river is partially frozen, but it is still flowing. The snow falls outside our windows, but we are safe and warm inside. We don't have to get the car out and go slip-sliding down the street. There is nowhere else that we have to be. We can shovel the walks after the first three inches fall. No need to wait for heart-attack-inviting shoveling. Or we can call the neighbor boy and watch him happily shovel his way to twenty dollars.

Whether we are going with the flow or against it, there is a price. When you are consistently headed in the opposite direction, you miss the comfort of company. If you are not in the flock, you can't expect the flock's protection. You risk the danger of being wrong. We ignore the wisdom of the mainstream at our peril. A third price that a life of swimming upstream tempts one to is smug self-righteousness. It is very tempting to imagine that I am right and you are wrong when the real truth might be that we have simply chosen different ways.

We acknowledge all the dangers of swimming against the flow. Nevertheless! Nevertheless, there is all this exuberance and

Saturday's child works hard for a living.

joy. I didn't get dressed today. I didn't even take a shower. Since awakening I have worked on projects I deeply care about. I am elated. Joy is surely freedom to do what you want, unbound from the chains of convention, to go against the flow.

> *Thank you for the great river of belonging in which we swim and for the freedom to explore both backwaters and branching streams. Teach us an appropriate humility that knows we are all afloat on the current of your love. Amen.*

*But the child born on the Sabbath day
is bright and blithe and bonny and gay.*

Sunday

gigo

JOHN 4:31 – 38

The title of this piece comes from the early days of computer programming. *GIGO* means "Garbage In, Garbage Out." As we listen to folks tell us about their many money problems, we see that they are often suffering from GIGO. Many of us look at our financial lives exactly wrong. We either look at our bills and try to figure out how to pay them, or we look at our income and try to find ways of making it grow.

Here's a secret. Financial well-being does not depend upon either income or outgo. As Dickens said in *David Copperfield*, what determines financial well-being is the relationship between the two. Here's Mr. Micawber's exact formula:

If income is X + 1 cent and outgo is X, the result is wealth.
If income is X − 1 cent and outgo is X, the result is poverty.

In other words, the only thing you have to worry about is the balance of income and outgo. This simple understanding is at the heart of living well financially.

But the child born on the Sabbath day is bright and blithe and bonny and gay.

So don't begin (as some budget counselors advise) looking at your current situation. Begin instead with your desires. While you are thinking, remember these five truths. First, everything has a cost, but, secondly, not all costs are monetary. Thirdly, it is true that "time is money," but fourth, time is much more precious and cannot be accumulated. The fifth truth is perhaps the most profound: We are limited creatures; we cannot have everything.

So make a list. What do you want? Be as specific as you can, and involve your whole family. After everybody has completed their lists, put all the items together. Then comes the hard part. You must rank the items on the master list in terms of importance. Do you see what happens? You discover a division between your wants and your needs. Down lower on the list, if you've done a good job of constructing it, is another division. You learn what you really want and what you only wish you had. If you cannot see either or both of those lines clearly, you might want to go back and revise your list before moving to step two.

The second step is to count the cost of each item on your list. Make separate columns for money costs, time costs, and costs that are expressed in some form other than money or time. This third column is the tricky one. If I say, for example, that I really want to be a professional football player, I am going to have some costs that will be expressed in terms of health and fitness.

If you have actually done the things suggested so far, your eyes have probably been opened more than once. Some things we want are in terrible tension with some other things. For example, high on our list is the ability to go to bed whenever we are tired and to wake up whenever we want to. This desire cannot possibly be realized if we commit ourselves to a nine-to-five job.

But the child born on the Sabbath day is bright and blithe and bonny and gay.

Another of our desires is to be home most of the time. One implication (another word for "price" or "cost") of this desire is clear: We cannot get much involved in activities that require spending a lot of time on airplanes.

At the beginning of this kind of thinking you may stumble a bit. It is easy to say, for instance, "Well, I can't have that; it's not how the world is." Don't settle for that superficial analysis. The truth is that we have a great deal of power and freedom to create the kind of world we want, if only we are willing to pay the prices for our choices.

Finally, try to separate what you really want from what you think you should want. Delay as long as possible any judgments that "this isn't right; it's not responsible." Those restraints—at least the real ones—will come along soon enough. Keep your eyes on what you really want and believe.

Much of our "poor talk" and fretting about "making ends meet" is just so much junk cluttering up our minds. Remember Mr. Micawber's wisdom. As long as we have that one cent more income than outgo, we are in the black. If we spend less time worrying about what we don't have, we'll have more gratitude for our blessing and energy to pursue what is truly valuable.

> *Thank you, God, for all the power we have. Thank you for making us with the ability to choose what we want and even, in some measure, what we need. Help us choose wisely so that we are glad to pay the prices for our choices. Amen.*

Monday

Monday's child is fair of face.

Location! Location! Location!

LUKE 19:41–44

Let's talk about suburbia's dirty little secret—drugs and crime. People often move to the suburbs because they think they can escape the "evils of the city." They want the space and privacy the suburbs promise, but those very qualities work against them. The distance and anonymity that seem so attractive obscure both the operations of the Outlaws motorcycle gang and the methamphetamine epidemic among suburban teens. All looks well on the surface of the suburbs—attractive lawns, homes, well-dressed children, and SUVs in the driveways. As with so much in life, however, the idyllic picture doesn't tell the whole story.

We moved from suburban Kuhberg to the inner city. Sixteen years ago we settled into a neighborhood of cozy bungalows on a one-block-long street on the edge of a little park. A main artery one block north connects us to bus lines or the freeway and downtown. While others may try to escape the city, we delight in it. Most of all we love the diversity of the people. On our block

Monday's child is fair of face.

alone there are African-Americans, Euro-Americans, and families from two distinct Hispano-American cultures.

Our move made economic sense as well. Our house is snugly well-constructed. Built in the 1920s, it has Spanish plaster walls and oak woodwork. It was recently assessed at $50,000. The same house, if it were available in the near suburbs, would cost over $100,000. In the farther suburbs it would be $200,000 or more. The streets here in the city are paved, and all utilities are in place. Our water-sewer bill is about a third of our friends' in nearby towns. Suburbanites demand the same services as city dwellers. In new suburban tracts, sewer and water lines must be laid and streets constructed. Suburban residents pay for their new infrastructure with higher tax and utility bills. Our taxes last year were just over $1,200, about a third of what comparable Kuhberg homeowners pay.

In Kuhberg many folks cut their lawns with garden tractors. The chore takes them most of the day. We have a lot and a half. There is lawn to mow; but it takes only about half an hour, using an electric mower. We have room for shady trees and both flower and vegetable gardens.

We have traded the illusions of the suburbs for the actual joys of the city. How do we love urban living? Let us count the ways.

Shortly after we moved to Milwaukee, Loren, one of our relatives, visited. Looking out the window Loren said, in a hushed voice betraying both horror and fascination, "Do you know there are Negroes in this neighborhood?"

"Of course we know," we replied. "That's one of the reasons we moved here."

Monday's child is fair of face.

We moved from the suburbs because we needed differentness. We had lived near the church in suburban Kuhberg because it was convenient. We assumed that was how it had to be. We realized it was time to move when one day in the supermarket we saw someone of a different ethnicity and stared in wonder. Too much sameness had taken its toll.

Our ethnically diverse neighbors are wonderful. Immediately to the north is an African-American family that moved in about six years ago; immediately south, a Cuban family who arrived two years later. When it snows, we have a friendly rivalry to see who can shovel the other's walks first.

Down the alley is an elderly German-American woman, who wags her head sometimes at the fact that the neighborhood is changing. She could easily move to a senior citizen's complex. Nevertheless, though she sometimes complains, she remains.

So do we, reveling in our little urban community. We amble through our park. We wave to neighbors as we walk to the library, post office, and neighborhood stores. If we still lived in Kuhberg, we would need to drive everywhere, isolated in our automobile. Our old friends in Kuhberg don't know what they're missing.

> *Dear God, surely you love the city because of how great the invitation is to connect and cooperate. Protect your cities, O God. Protect your people, and grant us your peace. Amen.*

Tuesday's child is full of grace. **Tuesday**

Eating Ethnic

LUKE 14:7–14

Does eating out mean your best clothes, reservations, a long wait, and a big check at the end? If so, it is time for an experiment. Some say that USAmerica is a melting pot. Others, a salad bowl. One thing is sure. It is a land of great ethnic diversity. A wonderful way to sample this variety is to be venturesome and eat ethnic. Of course, it is possible to dine lavishly at very expensive ethnic restaurants, but we have in mind the modest little places that pop up when people are beginning their life in USAmerica.

The best soup in the world, for example, is served somewhere in St. Paul. We don't know exactly where because we were momentarily lost when we stumbled in the door. "Hole in the wall" does not do it justice. The only attractive visual feature was cleanliness. The plates were old and worn as was the linoleum floor, but that little restaurant was clean.

And the smells were heaven. The aroma was what drew us in. Nothing that smells that wonderful can be anything but good. We never discovered the particular ethnicity of this restaurant.

Tuesday's child is full of grace.

Southeast Asian, we know, but whether Lao, Vietnamese, Hmong, or something else we cannot say because neither the proprietor nor the cook spoke enough English to communicate the country they called home.

Leek soup was the first course. At least we think they were leeks, seasoned with fresh basil. In the middle of winter! Where did he get that fresh basil and those abundant bean sprouts in the middle of a Minnesota winter? Chicken and rice was the main course, and there was some sort of fragile little honey thing for dessert.

Great food, wonderful hospitality, and then the bill. Often, one of the delights of dining in authentic ethnic restaurants is the bill. Two complete meals, as much as we could eat with offers of seconds on everything, and the check came to under ten dollars. For both of us! Two complete meals. We put a five on the table and would have left more if we hadn't thought it ridiculous to tip more than fifty percent.

That same trip to the Twin Cities was the first time we had Ethiopian food. It featured *injera*, a sort of sponge bread that was elastic and served as both plate and spoon. Good as the food was, the most enjoyable part of the experience was what it often is in ethnic restaurants. The staff is so eager to share their culture you wind up feeling more like guests than customers.

Chi Chi's and Taco Bell have predictability on their side. Judging from the menus of these chains, one might expect homogenized Mexican cuisine, but authentic Hispanic restaurants offer a palate-tickling surprise. Tex-Mex is vastly different from the cooking of Vera Cruz. While the Spanish tongue remains constant, the palate, like the accent, changes from place to place. Peruvian cookery is different from Puerto Rican. It's all

Tuesday's child is full of grace.

Hispanic, to be sure, but each region has its own unique character and flavor.

The delight of difference is surely a major reason to eat ethnic, so we'll keep looking for those holes in the wall where the food is an adventure and the welcome makes us think that we really might be at one big human family feast after all.

> *Thank you, God, for the diversity of your creation. Thank you for blessing us with such wondrous variety. Help us savor your unchanging love and mercy in the many meals with which you feed your many different peoples. Amen.*

Wednesday

Wednesday's child is full of woe.

As Simple as Black and White

ACTS 8:26–31

Can something as evil as racism be simplified? Perhaps so. Our congregation, Broken Walls Christian Community, is quite small but also quite thoroughly integrated. In the summer of 1998, I drove two little African-American girls from Broken Walls up to the denominational camp. They were six and seven at the time, and they were two of only four African-Americans at that camp session although in our judicatory African-Americans comprise about thirty percent of the fellowship.

When their week was over, I went back to get them and overheard a very poignant conversation. Although the girls had had a very good time at camp, although they swam and played and made friends, they were vaguely dissatisfied by the experience. In the back seat of my car, on the way home, they expressed to each other their dissatisfaction.

"There weren't enough black people in camp for me," Lakisha said to Cassandra. "What do you think?"

"Nope, me neither," Cassandra replied. "I had a lot of fun, but I didn't really feel—well, you know—comfortable."

Wednesday's child is full of woe.

I thought the little girls' conversation was so compelling that anyone and everyone would be able to understand that white racism really is a problem in modern USAmerica, but I was wrong. I told the girls' story in an op-ed piece that ran in the *Christian Science Monitor* and then sat back hoping to discover that I had done some good.

What I discovered instead is that some folks aren't affected even by the testimony of innocence. Given my Christian faith and what happened to Jesus, I don't know why I was surprised, but I was. Few of the folks who wrote me were crude or blatantly offensive, but the vast majority couldn't see that anyone had a problem—except me, of course, and the two little girls.

One of my correspondents wrote, "It saddens me that you've been gulled by the radical left. Don't you see those girls are already victims? The very fact of their complaining proves it." Another wrote, "You missed the opportunity. You should have reminded the girls that you were white and you loved them. With their attitude, all they're going to find in the world is trouble."

Despite the twisted "logic" of such persons, I nevertheless claim that even the evils of racism can be simplified, and here's why. In 1993, Virgilia, a woman in the Broken Walls congregation, took a sixteen-year-old out of the county jail and moved him into her home. Emmanuel was a street kid, and Virgilia decided he needed a father as well as a mom. Since there was not a long line of applicants, I accepted the position, and Emmanuel became my son.

For the next two-and-a-half years, we did everything fathers and adolescent sons do. We fought about school, rules, clothes, bedtime, and many other things. We also came to love each other—so much that one day, when we were having one of our

Wednesday's child is full of woe.

heated discussions, Emmanuel screamed, "I hate you, you ***ing white devil."

And then there was silence. And then there was a long, quiet conversation, and then there were tears—from both sides—and a long heartfelt hug.

It's not easy, but it really is simple. The way to overcome racism is for folks to get to know and love each other. All that needs to happen is that a white person and a black person come to love each other enough to dare to tell the truth, and then get over it. The same thing will need to happen, of course, with another pair of persons and then another and another and another.

But if we keep at it long enough, we will see each other not as different colors but as people, sisters and brothers, and children of God.

For Lakisha and Cassandra, after all, I am neither black nor white nor purple. I am simply Pastor David. For Emmanuel, by the grace of God, I am Dad.

> *Gracious God, forgive how we grieve you with our foolish angers and separations. Will your patience endure as we work out this terrible bitterness one relationship at a time? May it be so, in Jesus' name. Amen.*

Thursday's child has far to go. **Thursday**

The Necessities of Life

MATTHEW 6:7–13

Darlene entertains me in her living room of modern black lacquered furniture and white shag carpeting. Life is very difficult, she says. Everything is going wrong. Her income is next to nothing because her soon-to-be-ex-husband will not agree to reasonable alimony. Her life "is very hard," and what's more she doesn't have the "necessities of life."

Vinnie, on the other hand, lives in the old family farmhouse. For many years she cared for her bedridden husband. Shortly after his funeral I pay a call. A tiny, birdlike figure, she sits on the open oven door of her wood burning range. Peering at me through the thick lenses she wears after cataract surgery, she inquires if I would like a cup of coffee. She hobbles on bad hips to prepare it, offers cream and sugar, and places the cup down watching to see if all is to my liking.

What vastly different worlds these two women inhabit, the one in her condominium, the other in her farmhouse. The one pointedly serves up fashionable canapés and complaints. The other dispenses hospitality and is grateful for a visitor.

Thursday's child has far to go.

I sit on the leather sectional sofa contemplating the "necessities of life." Darlene reminds me of "our Christian obligation to provide for her needs. After all, don't Christians talk about caring for others as Jesus would have done?" Haven't I often spoken of "the importance of putting our faith into action"?

So I ask Darlene, "What are the necessities of life?"

For Vinnie, the necessities are wood for her stove, "food in the icebox," and an occasional visitor to chat with when you get lonely. She tells that her daughter-in-law is coming by with some groceries this afternoon; and Albert Jr. is going to put caulk around the front room windows for the winter. "They're so good to me. They take such good care of me," she says. "Everybody is so kind."

Our contentment and dissatisfaction are attitudes of the heart and will. If we have food and shelter and can enjoy the company of friends and family, then we are blessed. Unfortunately, not everyone—Darlene, for example—agrees.

"The necessities of life!" Darlene exclaims. "I don't have life's necessities."

"What are life's necessities?" I ask.

"At least these," Darlene says. "A computer, a VCR, and a microwave."

Two women, two vastly different worlds. The one looks for what she lacks and is miserable. The other sees what she has and rejoices.

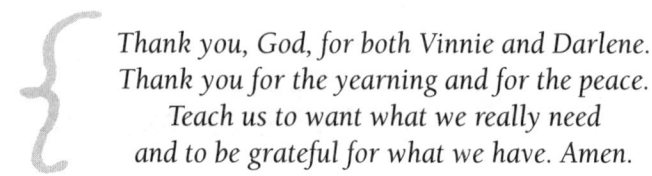

> *Thank you, God, for both Vinnie and Darlene.*
> *Thank you for the yearning and for the peace.*
> *Teach us to want what we really need*
> *and to be grateful for what we have. Amen.*

Friday's child is loving and giving. **Friday**

Recipe for Lemonade

ROMANS 12:9–17

Broken Walls Christian Community is a small, experimental congregation in the inner city. One of the best things that ever happened to us came as the skewed result of a good deed gone wrong. At the time of this story we were operating from a former parsonage. We didn't have much money (our annual budget never got above $8,000). Given the shoe-string character of our operation, we had made cosmetic improvements to the building, but anything more substantial was beyond our means. What we did have was space. Upstairs was an entire self-contained apartment complete with kitchen, bathroom, and private entrance.

One of our sister churches, Nethergrove Memorial, adopted a refugee family. The congregation embraced the family with enthusiasm. They took an active interest in their welfare, clothed them, fed them, found them jobs. The pastor was able to interest the local paper in the family's story of harrowing escape a hair's breadth ahead of national upheaval. Everyone got good

Friday's child is loving and giving.

publicity. The family was very brave, the congregation was very compassionate, and the community applauded.

At a gathering of clergy, the pastor of Nethergrove Memorial announced that this family of displaced persons no longer qualified for emergency shelter. I volunteered the use of the upstairs apartment "just as temporary quarters until they can find more suitable accommodations." Nethergrove Memorial members came in work crews to renovate the apartment. They mopped and scrubbed, painted and insulated. The congregation took to their mission project with admirable zeal, and the family moved in.

Hints that all was not well quickly accumulated. Dirty dishes piled up in the "church" kitchen sink. The "church" bathroom was unexpectedly festooned with pink curtains and fluffy rugs. One morning we arrived for worship to discover that a huge chest freezer had taken up residence in the downstairs kitchen. Friends of the family entered through the church entrance during church meetings and passed on into the family's apartment. Christmas Eve service began in competition with a radio blasting from an upstairs bedroom.

There were many experiences that produced friction—drains clogged with bacon grease, toilets plugged by mysterious objects, foreign-language graffiti in paint from the church cupboard. We attributed the incidents to "cross-cultural differences" or "the inevitable result of sharing space."

One of Nethergrove's members, Mr. Barry, became the family's champion. Whenever we raised a concern, Mr. Barry quickly chastised us for our insensitivity to the family's situation. They needed sympathy and understanding; we were being "judgmental" and "unreasonable."

Friday's child is loving and giving.

Six months came and went. Nine months. The family made no efforts at relocation. Clearly, they were here to stay. And then we got a phone call. "The parsonage is the property of the judicatory. You have been using the facility at our sufferance. The judicatory intends to disengage from the real estate business. How long will it take you to find another space?

"But what about the family?" we asked.

"Oh, no problem. We are giving the building to Nethergrove Memorial. They'll take care of them."

Although Nethergrove Memorial treated the family as a charity case, in their own country they ranked among the power elite. We found dishes in the sink, bacon grease down the drain, and dirty clothes strewn throughout our sanctuary because everyone in the family was accustomed to the ministrations of a household staff. These weren't needy people. They were privileged people who had lost a political struggle.

Nethergrove Memorial had misdirected its altruism. These people were not without resources. They would have been able to reestablish themselves anywhere. They were not part of the eighty percent of the world's population who live in substandard housing, nor part of the seventy percent unable to read, nor among the fifty percent suffering from malnutrition. The parents of the family are among the one percent of the world's people who are college educated. Ironically, Nethergrove Memorial was underwriting upper class persons. Their charity case came from a higher social strata than they themselves.

You might expect—and indeed for a while we felt—that the moral of this story was, "No good deed goes unpunished." Quickly, however, Broken Walls chose another maxim: "When life gives you lemons make lemonade." Although it's true we

Friday's child is loving and giving.

were out of the loop and out of the building, we were not out of ideas. Goodness came from this experience. We were freed from the albatross of building maintenance and freed, too, from our preconceptions about "doing church." As a result, we now travel to worship with folks who would not have Sunday morning services otherwise—a residential treatment center for mentally challenged adults and an inner-city nursing home.

Join us in a toast as we raise a tall, cool glass of lemonade in tribute to a good deed gone bad.

> *It's true, good God. All things do work together for those who trust you. Lead us into deeper levels of trust. You know better than we what is good for us. Choose what is best. Amen.*

Saturday's child works hard for a living. **Saturday**

Let the Housework Go

Luke 10:38–42

Let's share three secrets. The first is that housework is not very important. The second is that only a few of us know that housework is not very important. The last secret is that the housework that is important is not very hard.

My goodness, after a beginning like that, what more can we say? There certainly are not very many dusty corners left to run to and hide in. Too many cobwebs have been swept away. If these secrets are true, however, a big mystery remains. Why have so many women, over such a long time, complained so much about housework?

The short answer is that women have been sold a bill of goods. They have been told that the reason they are alive is to take care of men and children; that their job is to keep a spotless home. Folks have even used the Bible and the authority of Jesus to promote such nonsense, but the story of Mary and Martha tells us what Jesus really has to say.

Of course, there are some minor reasons that housework seems so hard. One is that it spreads itself out over the day.

Saturday's child works hard for a living.

There's no punching out at the end of the shift and punching back in sixteen hours later. The second little explanation is space. Folks who do housework are hardly ever absent from their jobs. The living room they are relaxing in is the same living room they have just cleaned—and will soon be cleaning again. The table at which the satisfying meal has just been eaten is not many footsteps from the kitchen where that meal was prepared—and where cleanup will soon occur.

These small reasons are real. They accurately describe disadvantages of doing housework, but they remain minor. The big explanation is more involved and has two parts. First, we are terrified by emptiness. One of the most distressing things we can imagine is being completely free from obligation. We seldom admit such a thing. We may not even know it, but look how we behave on vacations. We typically fill every moment with things to do. How many miles can we drive before sunset? How many sights can we see before it is time to go home?

Secondly, and more seriously, many of us don't feel very good about who we are. There are lots of different ways to say this—low self-concepts, bad self-images, little self-esteem. We may not believe we are very valuable, but all our activity at least keeps us busy. Our busyness distracts us from what we are afraid to see.

Take a look at the housework scheduled for this week and judge for yourself. Just why do those cupboards need to be cleaned? What terrible thing is going to happen if you do not scrub the kitchen floor?

Hearing no answer, we make a suggestion. Let the cupboard go and let the floor go too. For one whole week, don't do any housework. Don't worry. You'll still have work; it just won't be housework. Your job will be to pay close attention to yourself.

Saturday's child works hard for a living.

What do you feel like in all this emptiness? What are your temptations?

Things are changing in modern USAmerica—some things anyway. It used to be that women buried themselves in their housework and men got lost in their jobs outside the home. When men retired, they often experienced a new kind of lostness; and, very often, they shortly died. Women, of course, went on—with still too much housework to do.

It just might be that there is something more important. It's possible that there is nothing in life more important than housework, but, then again, it is also possible that there just might be. There's hardly a chance in a hundred, though, that we shall ever find our way to that greater value if we keep living chained to our chores.

If you're overburdened with housework, the only way you'll ever discover if there is anything more valuable is to take a chance. Maybe you can't manage a week, but how about three days? Let the housework go, and then pay attention to you.

> *Thank you for the story of Mary and Martha, dear God. Thank you for being so very clear about what matters. Thank you especially for the word of freedom to women, who are thirsting to hear it. Give us the courage to believe you and live in meaning, power, and joy. Amen.*

Sunday

*But the child born on the Sabbath day
is bright and blithe and bonny and gay.*

Boom, Thump, Tweet, Zing!

PSALM 150

Times have changed. It used to be that people made music, not just listened to it.

People no longer sing. They listen to the radio, CDs, and tapes. They watch music videos. Even music textbooks come with CDs so students can hear the music they are studying. We think it's a tragic loss.

Throughout history, people, even under the most deprived conditions, have improved their lot by making music. Harry Belafonte's "Day-O" is an example of work songs developed by laborers to ease their burdens. African-Americans under slavery made "Juba" (from "jubilation") by using their bodies as percussion accompaniment to singing. Without any other resources beyond themselves, they created art.

Making music brings joy. Vibrations of tone fill us with vitality. Rhythm is a pulsing heartbeat under the tune. We discover order in the patterns of notes and silences. Then within the pattern we become surprised. Singing, plinking, blowing, and thumping are spiritually illuminating. As we find our way into

But the child born on the Sabbath day is bright and blithe and bonny and gay.

the center of a clear, pure tone of dead-certain pitch, our hearts confirm the truth that "God gave us music so we could pray without words." The beautiful sound is its own reward.

The spiritual discipline of music makes us want not to turn the page of the etude book until the exercise is artfully played. Practice is not punishment but an upward spiral into the nonverbal truths of music. Growth in skill and mastery is observable and measurable. We begin unable to produce a single proper tone but now can play a scale. We take the exercise very slowly at first; then easily at a much faster tempo.

The spiritual discipline of music teaches the virtue of consistency. Effective practice requires regularity and focus. One must keep count while maintaining proper position, tone production, and pitch. This process teaches self-examination and self-critique. We confront the truth about our playing. Am I ready to turn the page? Ought I to stay with this exercise and work some more?

One of the most valuable lessons that music making teaches is patience with the process. We are all on a journey, with some further ahead and others lagging behind. What matters is where we're headed, not the speed at which we are traveling. It's the process, not just the product, that is valuable. We discover that whenever we are making music, music brings us joy.

If this all makes sense to you—but more especially if it doesn't—there is a book you really ought to read. It's *The Listening Book* by W. A. Mathieu, Shambhala: Boston; 1991. Be kind to yourself and buy a copy. After it has changed you—perhaps even transformed you—don't forget to pass it on.

But the child born on the Sabbath day is bright and blithe and bonny and gay.

> *Thank you, God, for the mystery of music. Thank you for rhythm, pitch, and tone. Give us the courage to be more than passive lumps that neither listen nor hear. Then give us the delight of making music of our own. Amen.*

Monday's child is fair of face.   **Monday**

Such a Steal!

Hebrews 12:14–17

Modern culture says, "Sell yourself short and buy some self-worth." We are bombarded with messages that say, "Pay more, get more. If you can afford it, why not enjoy?" But the more money we have, the more our desires expand. Our wants are inexhaustible. How much is enough? What is too much?

Aunt Sally was rhapsodizing the other day about a bargain she had found. Uncle Bob is a very particular man. He likes his clothes, especially his shirts, just so.

"All cotton of course," Sally said. "A little extra moving room through the shoulders, and cuffs falling at exactly thirty-four-and-a-half inches. It's hard to find the shirts he likes," Sally said, "but I did, only a couple of weeks ago, and such a deal. Only $65. In lots of three or more, only $62.95."

Aunt Sally and Uncle Bob own a condo with a fabulous view of the lakefront. They shoot breathtaking photos of sunrise on the water right from their balcony. In addition to the great view,

Monday's child is fair of face.

their monthly fee of $2,800 buys such amenities as the services of a concierge.

Jimmy wouldn't recognize the word *concierge*. He lives in public housing. His big brother Antony gives him $20 every week or so. Jimmy can hardly wait for his allowance. He rushes right over to Sweet's Treats and buys candy. Then he goes to the Hip-Hop Shop and buys a new CD. If there's any money left, Jimmy will go to Burger Blaster and get an order of hot fries and a large Coke. In a little under three hours, Jimmy has spent his $20. Soon the CD will be scratched because Jimmy will grow tired of it and forget to put it back in the case. Shortly thereafter, his little sister will step on the case and break it. No problem. Antony will give Jimmy more money next week.

The two sets of circumstances are greatly different, but all four characters in these stories share a common perception. Both Sally and Antony are trying to buy gratification for Bob and Jimmy. The question for the rest of us is, how might we be trying to buy our satisfaction?

Glossy magazines tell us how to look. TV hypnotizes us into wanting whatever is being sold. Our friends and neighbors shop till they drop, and we don't want to be left behind. We try to keep up with trends, but it is a costly and never-ending race. We are never ahead of the latest fashion wave and always chasing an illusion.

Just because I can afford something doesn't mean I should buy it. Life is precious. We cannot afford to waste it in the vain pursuit of trinkets and baubles. The ceaseless cycle of want-shop-buy needs to stop. Prior to any shopping expedition we are invited to rethink the meaning of "discretionary income." We

Monday's child is fair of face.

can make some distinctions. Is this something I need? Want real bad? Saw on TV and thought I'd get one?

Although our wants are inexhaustible, our needs are really few. When we really need a hug, we should not settle for new shoes or a table saw. When we need someone to listen, we cheat ourselves by choosing a cruise instead. What good does an extra thousand square feet of living space do if the rooms are always empty? The things in themselves are not bad of course. It's just that they can't love us back.

To live, we need love, food, clothing, and shelter. Love costs nothing. The rest, with careful shopping, can be had for very little. Sadly, we settle for the pottage of appearance. We try to buy self-worth with all our shopping, but self-esteem cannot be bought and wrapped up in a box. If our priorities are not in order, we will spend money trying to buy what is actually free.

Whether we count our wealth in pennies or millions of dollars, the questions are the same. What are we shopping for? Are we buying what we really want? Need?

> *Thank you for the reminders of what real worth is, dear God. Help us separate what we want from what we need. Teach us not to try to buy what is really a gift from you. Amen.*

Tuesday

Tuesday's child is full of grace.

The Final Simplicity

ROMANS 8:35–39

Once upon a time, death was a reasonably simple affair. Most folks died at home in the care of their family, and after the dying was over, the women would wash and dress the body. There would be a very brief time to express immediate grief since no embalming happened and deterioration was quick, and then the remains went into the ground.

No longer. We now have ICUs with their ventilators and all the other machines that keep breath moving and blood flowing. For the end stages when only palliative care is possible, we have nursing homes and hospices, and doctors may be standing by to harvest everything from skin and corneas to kidneys and heart. When death finally happens, as it still inevitably does, we have a sophisticated and diverse funeral industry with options ranging from bronze casket to cremation. Death is no longer a simple affair.

A major implication for righteousness is that we pay more attention to our own death and dying. At bare minimum, we are invited to arrange the disposition of our bodies and the creation

Tuesday's child is full of grace.

of our memorial services. Whatever our decisions, we have the additional responsibility of communicating to our survivors our wants and desires and the actions we have taken.

The first step is to be as aware and proactive as possible about the health care we are receiving. Do you really want physical survival as long as possible no matter what? The three most recent funerals I have officiated at have been for persons who had a wide variety of answers. "Arthur," at seventy-three, was completely ready to die. He told his doctor, his daughter, and me that he wanted only to ease his pain, and he must have meant what he said, for he died even before he could be transferred from hospital to hospice, in fact, three days after his admittance.

"Bob," also seventy-three, represents something of a middle course. Bob suffered a massive stroke on Thursday evening and went immediately into a deep coma, so he wasn't able to tell his wife Mary what he wanted. Fortunately, they had spoken before in a theoretical way, and Bob had said repeatedly, "I wouldn't ever want to live hooked up to machines."

"Charlie," on the other hand, wanted to stay alive as long as possible at whatever cost. His desires were honored. Charlie died at the age of ninety-four after a long, slow decline.

The point of sketching the last days of these three men is not to claim that one made a better decision than the others. Rather each decided what was right for him, communicated that desire to his family, and had his wishes honored. Moreover, each man had the sort of memorial service that he had hoped to have.

Have you written a living will and spoken openly, honestly, and comprehensively with your physician? Does someone in your family know of your decision? Have you identified your personal representative to family and friends?

Tuesday's child is full of grace.

Do you have a will? Some of the ugliest disputes that ever happen in families center around the division of assets after someone dies. You have not only the right to distribute your wealth as you see fit but also the opportunity to ease potential strife among your survivors.

Have you met with a local funeral service and made arrangements, perhaps even prepaying for the services your family will receive? Your survivors will have enough to do with the grieving of your loss. You can spare them the added stress of such details as selecting a casket and tending to funeral arrangements.

When we are willing to discharge this final set of responsibilities, we sometimes notice an unanticipated benefit. Serious conversation with loved ones about such solemn matters can create an atmosphere of openness and sharing. As is always true, our preparations for the future are tested for their rightness and righteousness by the differences they make in our circumstances and relationships right here and now.

> *Thank you, God, for the fact of my death.*
> *Thank you that I do not have forever and that*
> *I have the power to live well and prepare for*
> *a good dying. Thank you for the deep reminder*
> *that we are all utterly at your mercy, which*
> *is the best place possible for us to be. Amen.*

Wednesday's child is full of woe. **Wednesday**

If It Feels Good . . .

ROMANS 7:14–19

When little children stand at the windows of old houses in the inner city, their lips rest at sill level. They lick and taste—sweet! They peel paint chips and eat. It tastes good. Unfortunately, many old houses were painted with lead-based paint. When the children eat the deliciously sweet paint, they poison themselves. The treatment for lead poisoning is a painful process called chelation. All the blood from one's body must be drained and purified of lead before it can be returned to the circulatory system. The small pleasure of a little sweetness exacts a large price.

Nevertheless, I know a lot of lead-eaters, including myself. We know what we're doing isn't good for us but do it anyway— bad habits, overindulgence, hurtful relationships, addictions. We seem unable to distinguish what is bad but seductive from what is truly good. I, for example, have a perverse passion for cheese curls. I have eaten myself sick with an entire bag of them. Afterward I felt greasy, queasy, and unsatisfied—not to mention being stained with tell-tale orange-dyed fingers.

Wednesday's child is full of woe.

We lead eaters cussedly compound our problems. We choose not to do what we know is good for us—read more, exercise, eat healthful foods. How many walks in the park have we passed up because it was easier to stay inside? We avidly avoid good things while we poison ourselves with imagined impunity. The cure is spiritual chelation, discovering what is really good for us. Ah, and then—this is the hard part—doing it.

We adopt behaviors because they once worked. They made us feel good or helped us cope. The difficulties come when we continue the behavior beyond its usefulness. Brooding silence may once have challenged parental authority. In the present, however, pouting impedes problem solving. Mom or Dad may have acquiesced to a protruding lower lip, but one's spouse or colleagues will judge such tactics simply immature.

Causes may be complex and roots deep. We may need to name them clearly, but naming isn't changing. As the joke about Freudian therapy says, "I was in analysis for twenty years. I didn't get any better; but now I really know my neuroses." Real change is difficult. We get used to our ruts—even, in some strange way, learn to like them.

When I was a child, my mother was forever putting me on one diet after another. I always felt deprived—and hungry. I wanted Twinkies, chips, candy (and cheese curls!) in my lunch, just like the lunches other kids had. I hated the carrot and celery sticks that appeared in my lunchbox. It has taken me years to believe that eating well is not the problem, nor is dieting the path to happiness and self-acceptance. I don't eat Twinkies now because I find their Styrofoam texture offensive. I eat carrots and celery now not because I am compelled to but because I actually like vegetables.

Wednesday's child is full of woe.

What changed? My taste buds? Maybe. More likely, though, it was my attitude. I read the ingredients on the Twinkies label for myself and concluded that plastic is not one of the nutritional elements of good health. Veggies appear more attractive in terms of color, crunch, vitamin content, and fiber. Most of all, I have figured out that really loving and caring for the body God gave me means doing what is good for me, not what masquerades as goodness but is lead paint in disguise.

> *Gracious God, help us choose what is truly best for us. You know what we really need. May we trust enough to welcome your wisdom. Give us your desire for our lives. Amen.*

Thursday

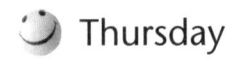

Thursday's child has far to go.

Thinking about Money

PHILIPPIANS 3:7–11

As I often tell my college writing students, we human beings do not think very often. Most of the time we feel or assume, but genuine thinking is rare. This business of what "thinking" really means reminds me of Jean Piaget and the work he did early in the twentieth century with the developmental psychology of children. Piaget is famous for his conversations with little children about whether the moon could be called "sun" and the sun "moon."

The children thought the matter a big joke. "Oh, no, Dr. Piaget," they protested. "Of course the sun is the sun and the moon's the moon. How else could it be?" The children were completely incapable of conceiving of the arbitrary quality of language. In that inability they were not so different from many other human beings much older than they.

Ask most folks to determine the monetary value of an object, and they will try to come up with "the right answer." If the object they are appraising is a familiar one and if their knowledge of the market is current, the answer they arrive at will be very close to

Thursday's child has far to go.

"correct." What most folks don't consider, however, is how conventional all such meanings are. "Conventional"—I mean the word quite literally. The monetary value of anything is simply an expression of agreement between those who have the object and those who want it. "What is it worth?" is always answered most efficiently and effectively by means of determining what it will bring in the marketplace.

So let's think as Christians.

One possibility is that Christian reflection upon economics is identical to secular reflection. Much of the book of Deuteronomy reflects this sort of thinking. Material wealth exists in a positive and direct correlation with righteousness. Obey God and prosper. Puritan New England in American Colonial times is a typical expression of this kind of thinking.

A second possibility is that the two systems of value are completely opposite. According to economics, desires are relatively unlimited, but the means to satisfy those desires are very limited indeed. This scarcity means that every situation finally comes down to "if you get more, I must have less." In the "economy of love," however, the more I give, the more I get. Love is unlimited, and love is the only thing of real value. Therefore ignore the way the world measures worth, and follow the path of love.

There are two other possibilities, both combinations of these first two. Following Luther and his theory of Two Kingdoms, it may be that the two "economic" systems are opposite but not in tension with one another, so the appropriate thing to do is respond to each on its own terms. When living in the world, one should obey the rules of the economy of scarcity. When relating to God, however, one should follow the principles of the economy of love.

Thursday's child has far to go.

The last possibility is the most dynamic and ambiguous. Perhaps all three conceptions, (Deuteronomistic, Economy of Love, Two Kingdoms) are both true and false. Maybe it depends upon situation and circumstance. Sometimes, for example, financial wealth may be a sign of obedience to God and the blessing that results, but at other times a saintly person, perhaps even the same person, may live in dire poverty. In a particular situation, both sets of principles may be applying simultaneously, and the way of wisdom is to tell how much, which, when.

One of the most interesting and frustrating things about thinking is its inconclusiveness. Each resolution poses new issues, and the process continues until we run out of either energy or time. There are no final answers. We are never finished; we simply stop. Everything is provisional and grist for the mental mill. This open-endedness of the rational process may be one of the major reasons for its disuse. Most folks want answers they can trust and then to be done.

Careful thinking leads mostly to more thinking.

But the great commandment, Jesus says, the *greatest* commandment, is to love God with heart, soul, mind, and strength—with, in fact, our whole selves. So we make a beginning and plod on believing that when we have run out of strength, God will be there at the end to make up all our shortfalls.

> *May it be so, Lord Jesus. Please honor our little efforts to make sense of your creation, and tune us with your wisdom so that we know when to think, when to quit, and through it all to have the willingness to wait upon you. Amen.*

Friday's child is loving and giving. **Friday**

How Many Cars Do We Need?

ECCLESIASTES 5:10–12

USAmerica is in love with its cars, but like all love affairs, this one is not entirely rational. Some advertisements, for example, say that buying a new car is "an investment." Of course not, or if it is, it is a very bad investment indeed. As soon as one drives a new car out of the dealership, it depreciates frighteningly. The fact is that cars are not investments; they are symbols—of freedom, power, and status. Early in our marriage, we decided that this is a game we do not want to play.

Nevertheless, like many USAmericans, we once thought we needed a car for every driver in the house. Schedules and destinations are different. If we can afford it, we said, why inconvenience ourselves? But then we got serious about setting the priorities of our lives and discovered that one car is enough for even three drivers. Some very interesting things happen when you restrict yourself to a single car.

The most obvious early benefits are financial. Drop a car from the insurance, and you almost halve the bill. It is very much like

Friday's child is loving and giving.

getting a raise. Owning only one car encourages making careful choices. Less driving means gasoline and maintenance costs also drop nearly in half. The benefits, however, are more than financial. They are also emotional, ecological, and even spiritual.

Many of the emotional benefits come from the sharing that happens when there is only one family car. In the summer, for example, we have a wonderful time. From 8:30 until 11:00 in the morning, Monday through Thursday, Lo-Ann needs to be up north in Brown Deer teaching a drama class. From 10:00 until noon on the same days, I teach writing down south in the city.

The solution is a piece of cake. I take some writing projects with me to occupy the early hours, and Lo-Ann takes a book and one of her musical instruments to occupy her while waiting for a ride. What seems like inconvenience becomes invitation for increased productivity. One summer we wrote most of a book in these six weeks of sharing the car. Increased productivity is nice, but a deeper benefit is the repeated reminder that we are a family.

The emotional benefit is seen to be spiritual when we realize that we are not merely independent individuals off on our own private journeys. We are connected to each other, dependent upon one another. For one car to work, everyone must cooperate. Those times when we have had children in our home are an even more powerful lesson in sharing, not only for us but also for the children. Each one learns that she is special enough to have some rights regarding transportation, but each one also learns that he must negotiate so that everyone's needs and desires are attended.

Naturally enough, the spiritual blessing reminds us of the ecological. When we own only a single car, we are being good not only to ourselves but also to society and to the natural envi-

Friday's child is loving and giving.

ronment. Such financial benefits as less fuel used and reduced maintenance are also ecological benefits too.

Sharing a single car has yet another surprising benefit. We discover that we talk more to each other. What better environment is there for a close conversation than closed up in a small space where there is not much else to do than make connection? Some folks turn on the radio (even watch TV) in the car, but we have discovered a much better practice is to ride along in silence. Inevitably, someone discovers they have something to say. The practice pays dividends even during short city hops, but long journeys sometimes produce some very deep sharing.

Sometimes having a single car doesn't work. There are spur-of-the-moment occasions when someone wants to go somewhere, but the car is gone. Times like these are when living in a city is a special blessing. Three bus lines are within easy walking distance, and those three routes connect us with the entire system. In a pinch, there are cabs. Even an occasional thirty-dollar cab ride looks pretty cheap when compared with the expense of maintaining an extra car.

Just when we think we have cataloged all the advantages to having a single car, along comes another surprise. We discover the financial savings have produced some extra discretionary income, and we are free to pursue some additional diversions. Sometimes, for example, I'd like a week off to visit family and friends, but Lo-Ann has projects here. I guess I'll rent a car, but I'll do it more economically than through Budget or Avis. I'll drive our car on vacation, and we'll call Rent-A-Wreck for Lo-Ann's car. It will probably cost about half the name brand rates, and the untested car, in case something happens to it, will be right here at home.

Friday's child is loving and giving.

{ *Thank you that the answer is not always more and bigger. Thank you for the invitation to live inside the limits of our lives, and for the joy and thanksgiving that come when we do. Amen.* }

Saturday's child works hard for a living. **Saturday**

Wanting It All

JOHN 15:8–16

Rusty is a delightful kid with a carrot-color butch haircut. He has a gift for music and an intense interest in computers. Rusty has also been diagnosed with ADHD, "Attention Deficit/ Hyperactivity Disorder." ADHD is typified by an inability to focus. People with ADHD live at a frenetic pace, often flitting from activity to activity, yet Rusty has some wisdom for us all.

We jam-cram-pack so much activity into our lives it's hard to tell when we have time to live. We juggle work, school, church, and community meetings with travel (for both job and leisure), the gym, self-improvement classes, and sports. Parents must fit their own appointments in among their children's soccer practices, music and dance lessons, forensics meets, field trips, and play dates. We want it all. We want it now. We don't want to choose. We are terribly afraid of missing out on any opportunity.

As a consequence of our over-commitment, others start setting our agendas. "You can't play on the team if you miss more than three practices." "Your evaluation will be seriously compromised

Saturday's child works hard for a living.

if you refuse to work the next four weekends." "You must attend the dress rehearsal or you cannot play the concert." We resent these imperious demands, but we have brought them on ourselves. We try to do everything because we resist choosing. Choosing means admitting our limitations. We simply can't do everything.

Let's listen to Rusty's wisdom.

> MUSIC TEACHER: Why don't you want to play in Saturday Ensemble?
> RUSTY: It's okay. I dunno. I like to sleep late on Saturday mornings.
> MUSIC TEACHER: You've got a wonderful ear.
> RUSTY: Yeah.
> MUSIC TEACHER: I just don't understand.
> RUSTY: I have tutoring during the week after school. It's too late to go play then. So Saturday morning is the only time I have just to mess around and play with my friends.

Rusty knows more about setting priorities than many supposedly normal folks three times his age. Rusty's got it right. We need time "just to mess around and play" with friends and family. All our scheduling and busyness can't replace the sheer delight of spontaneous fun. Perhaps Rusty has been misdiagnosed. It may be that our society has ADHD.

Perhaps in heaven we will be able to pursue all the good options we passed up on earth. In this life, however, we must choose. One good choice excludes another. Becoming executive vice president means increased status and higher pay, but it also means longer hours and less time with family. We choose what we most value.

Saturday's child works hard for a living.

We need to settle down and focus. The mind can give maximum attention to only one thing at a time. If someone says "pink Tunisian turnips" that image fills the mind. We pretend to "multi-task," but it is an illusion. We dilute, not enrich, our lives with too much activity. We can't enjoy one single thing because we aren't paying full attention. We are fussing about the next engagement or fixating on the whole host of commitments on our calendar. We have overbooked our pleasures. We live with attention deficit. We hyperactively seek new diversions. Let's stop at Rusty's side—to smell the roses, watch the clouds, taste the coffee, caress our loved ones, and savor life—one activity at a time.

> *God of Sabbath rest, help us stop the harried racing though our day. Open us to the wonder of your world. Slow us down to catch our breath that we might breathe deeply of your sweet Holy Spirit. Amen.*

Sunday

*But the child born on the Sabbath day
is bright and blithe and bonny and gay.*

Choose You This Day

JOSHUA 24:14–15

With money, as with all the rest of our lives, what it really comes down to is choosing. Everything else we do is preliminary and much less crucial. We develop, assess, and even critique our tastes. We identify our emotions and try to discover what they mean. We think as hard as we can (or want to), but then, finally, we must choose.

I'm reminded of the old Jack Benny joke. (Jack Benny, for you youngsters, was a much loved comedian of radio and early television days who made great sport of being the world's stingiest miser.) Periodically, Benny would be accosted by a robber, who demanded, "Your money or your life."

There was an exquisite pause, a very extended pause, and the robber would become impatient. "Well, which is it?" the robber demanded.

"I'm thinking," Benny replied. "I'm thinking."

So are we all, but, like Benny, what we are really doing is choosing. Four hours of overtime or attending our daughter's soccer game? A family outing to the zoo or working to bag this

But the child born on the Sabbath day is bright and blithe and bonny and gay.

new client? Hiding this income from the IRS or living with integrity?

Another way of asking the question, a way that perhaps makes it easier to know just what is at stake, is this: What is value? How does one determine what something is worth, and how can the various values be compared? We sometimes shrink from such questions because they are often loaded with blame. The implicit threat is, "You'd better choose correctly or else!"

Or else what? You'll be punished. You'll be a bad person. No one will love you. Your mother/family/friends will be disappointed in you. But what if responsibility is gift, not punishment? What if the only way our lives can have any genuine meaning is if we are free to choose?

We see the nature of responsibility by examining the parent-child relationship. Initially, the child's responsibility for her or his life is negligible, and the parents' responsibility for the child is almost total. Parental responsibility, however, is a diminishing arc over time. When my child is newly born, I am one hundred percent responsible for her. When he is six, perhaps ninety-five percent. At ten, maybe eighty-five percent. Somewhere in adolescence, my child and I exchange places in terms of who is more than half responsible for her life, and when they reach full adulthood, my responsibility approaches zero. It may well be that I have helped cause many of my child's problems even when he is in his forties, but cause is not responsibility.

This parent-child example is an extended way of stating a very simple fact. Persons are free moral agents. The only way life makes moral sense is if we are all responsible for our own choices and behaviors.

But the child born on the Sabbath day is bright and blithe and bonny and gay.

In terms of money it comes down to this. There are many competing notions about the importance of money and how much is "enough." We hear conflicting claims from various corners of our worlds. Financial advisors say, "You can never have too much money. The more cushion, the safer you'll be." After all, they have devoted their lives to wealth building and have more than a financial investment in the project. Since they have dedicated their time and energy to the accumulation of wealth, they must assure themselves of the significance of their efforts.

The vocabulary is different, but the claims are much the same from the players in the ghetto. They make their investments in big cars, heavy gold chains, and flashy clothes. They cultivate their image as smooth operators. They too believe, "You can't never have too much money. The bigger the roll, the better it go."

Jesus has a very different claim. "Foxes have holes and birds have nests, but the Son of Man has nowhere to lay his head." To the dream of amassing future wealth he responds, "This very night your soul will be required of you." When hypocritically challenged to advocate one authority over another, he says, "You must choose. Pay to Caesar what is Caesar's and to God what is God's."

Jesus doesn't put much stock in money's ability to ensure our futures. He does, however, greatly value the human capacity for choice. With his psychologist's insight he observes, "No one can serve two masters." With his servant heart he exhorts, "Lose your life for my sake and the gospel's." With his prophetic vision he cries, "Repent for the reign of heaven has come near." He consistently asserts that though money has its uses, place, and purpose, it cannot offer any genuine protection. Jesus chooses God every time as the ultimate hedge against the future.

But the child born on the Sabbath day is bright and blithe and bonny and gay.

In large measure, we are free to choose among the claims. We get to decide how important money is to us. It is exactly as important as we choose for it to be.

> *Thank you, God, for such an amazing level of trust. Thank you for granting us the wonderful gift of free will. Forgive our foolish choices and grant us the courage to embrace our freedom. Amen.*

Monday

Monday's child is fair of face.

Movies in Your Head

MATTHEW 6:22–23

Sometimes we go to the movies in the afternoon to take advantage of the lower prices, and sometimes we wait until the film makes its way to the budget theater. Since we don't have a television (see "Toss It Out!" if you're interested in that possibility), you might think us starved for visual entertainment, but you would be wrong.

In fact, our visual entertainment is state of the art. We are on the cutting edge of the technology and possess the most sophisticated visual entertainment hardware ever made. Moreover, it is not difficult to justify this extravagance. Most of the films we watch cost us nothing because we view them in our heads. Our state-of-the-art visual entertainment system is called "the human imagination," and it usually begins with books. A major form of entertainment at our house is reading aloud to each other.

Right now, we're working our way through Jane Austen—again. We just finished *Sense and Sensibility* and are about five chapters into *Pride and Prejudice*. Prior to Ms. Austen, we read

Monday's child is fair of face.

C.S. Lewis' *Chronicles of Narnia*, and before that, it was Tolkien's *Lord of the Rings*. Another favorite is Dorothy L. Sayers' Lord Peter Wimsey Mysteries.

Not only fiction is on our agenda. Jacques Barzun's *From Dawn to Decadence* is absolutely fascinating, and right now we're reading a little book on *Luther's Table Talk* (by Preserved Smith; isn't that a wonderful name?). There are so many advantages to this form of entertainment that they almost defy listing, much less explaining fully, but let's try.

We are completely free to read whatever we want, whenever we want. We are not at the mercy of release dates either in theaters or on tape. Moreover, we can move at our own pace. Three chapters tonight? Sure, why not? Skip an evening? Of course, no problem.

We can follow wherever our interests lead and then come back to the story. For instance, we recently became so interested in Sayers that we read two volumes of her letters and even bought some radio dramas (that we have yet to read). It's fun to share the experience with like-minded friends. We have convinced at least one other couple to read aloud to each other, and sometimes the four of us discuss a book we have all read.

Of course, we can read again anything that has really captivated us, and as we bring fresh energy and perspective, it's always a new adventure. This is just about the least expensive form of entertainment there is. Do you have any idea how many readings a well cared for copy of *The Complete Works of Jane Austen* can provide?

At this point in our lives, we are a couple living together alone, but if you have children or teenagers at home, the advantages of reading aloud to each other grow by leaps and bounds.

Monday's child is fair of face.

Sharing quality literature is not only enjoyable. The experience also presents many natural avenues for discussing important life issues. The sharing builds vocabulary, increases critical thinking skills, and introduces all participants to a bigger and more interesting world. Just remember to pick reading matter that everyone will enjoy, and if that restriction prevents you from reading something you really want to, who's to say that every member of the family must be present at every reading?

Especially when more than two people are reading, include some good dramas in your schedule. You might actually "block out" the action of some scenes and walk through them with books in hand, and don't forget poetry. Make sure you choose accessible poetry, and start with little doses. Poetry is very rich food, and a little goes a long way. One of the delights of reading poetry aloud is that it is exactly how it was intended to be read.

> *Thank you for our imaginations, dear God. Thank you that in large measure we can set the limits of our lives. Teach us to rejoice in our power to be co-creators with you. Amen.*

Tuesday's child is full of grace.

Tuesday

Keeping Christmas

Isaiah 9:6 – 7

I've always found it ironic that a people protesting the commercialization of Christmas should wear mass-produced buttons from Hallmark that say, "Keep Christ in Christmas." It is especially ironic when you know that Christ never left Christmas. We've just been looking in the wrong places. My yuletide tongue-clucking is tempered by the remarks of Lutheran theologian Joseph Sittler. Dr. Sittler observed, "We Christians shouldn't begrudge the world its tinseled Christmas. It's all they have." We have the real thing. If we look in the right places, we will discover that Christ is very much present.

Last year, I noticed the stores began holiday decorating just after Halloween. Christmas is one more peg upon which to hang a promotion, attract shoppers, and move merchandise. Not so at the Carters' house. To their neighbors, the Carters probably appear like Mr. and Mrs. Scrooge. During the four weeks preceding Christmas they do no decorating, hang no stockings. Instead, they get ready spiritually. They observe Advent ("coming").

Tuesday's child is full of grace.

Originally, Advent was called a little Lent. People once fasted and prayed to prepare to rightly welcome the Christ child. Weekly, they lit Advent candles and reflected on what Jesus' birth meant, and sang carols like this old German one:

> *At Advent time a candle burns.*
> *At Advent time a candle burns.*
> *First one, then, two, then three, then four;*
> *Then stands the Christ child at our door.*

With all the external trappings stripped away, one can better see whose coming it is.

When Christmas comes, the Carters are truly ready, but the stores are through with Christmas by Christmas Eve. The inventory goes on sale. Time to bring out the Valentines! Shoppers have had Muzak carols drilled into their ears until they are sick of them. Decorations have begun to look tatty. The world says it's all over. The Carters' celebration is just beginning.

We cast our lot with the Carters. The worship services on Christmas Eve and Christmas Day have become very precious to us. The candle-lit faces of worshipers reflect the hope of new life. Through them we see God's grace and mercy. Their glistening eyes shine with wonder in the silent, holy night. Christmas morning communion manifests the wonder of the Incarnation.

Some families open gifts on Christmas Eve, some on Christmas Day. We don't open our packages at all because we are counting the twelve days of Christmas. After four weeks of spartan Advent we want to prolong the party. In a delightful learning from our Latino kindred, we defer our family gift-giving until "Old Christmas," Epiphany. We watch the Magi traverse afar,

Tuesday's child is full of grace.

progressing from east to west, toward the crèche. Little homey rituals like these have become treasured traditions.

I remember hearing a man say after an Advent service, "I think it's terrible the way they commercialize Christmas. Well, gotta go. I've gotta buy my kids some more toys." The commercialism won't stop unless we stop. We see the Christ in Christmas ever more clearly as we free the manger from its swaddling bands of gift-wrapping, tissue paper, and ribbons. Christ is still there at the heart of it. He is simply waiting for us to seek him and when we find him, fall on our knees and worship.

> *Guide us by the light of Christ's star to worship at the manger. Aid us in unpacking Christmas meanings we need to keep and share. Amen.*

Wednesday

Wednesday's child is full of woe.

Grasping at Air

LUKE 12:16–21

The ads in the weekly news magazines are often just as fascinating as the editorial material. One headline, for example, screams, "Take Charge of Your Financial Future," and the subhead promises, "You do not have to be at the mercy of chance and change."

Be a disciplined saver, the ads urge. If you are, you can guarantee yourself a comfortable financial future. Of course, the advertisements remind us, it is also necessary to connect with competent professional advice, and one must begin early to "build a solid retirement plan."

It looks good—on paper. But paper can capture only the smallest fragment of the truth of life. In fact, there are two huge stumbling blocks in the way of assuring our financial future.

The first is that we do not know what lies ahead. The trends may continue, or they may not. The collapse of NASDAQ was not the first time a financial bubble burst. Back in the late 1970s, for example, one of my dearest friends, a life-long coin collector, made a very bad financial move. He thought he was being pru-

Wednesday's child is full of woe.

dent. He decided to buy gold and silver as a hedge for his other, "more volatile" investments.

Bill started buying when gold was just under $600 an ounce. It reached $800, and then the bottom fell out. A precipitous slide became a steady decline. In 2001, gold bottomed out at $255 an ounce. At the time of this writing, the figure is $345. These numbers mean that Bill's initial gold is now, thirty years after the original purchase, worth just about half what he paid for it, without, of course, adjusting for three decades of inflation.

The decline in the price of silver—Bill also bought silver, remember—has been even more dramatic. From a high of $55 an ounce in 1980, silver is now selling for about $4, a loss of significantly more than ninety percent.

So the first problem with attempting to secure the future is that we do not know what the future holds. The second problem is even more arresting. We may not have any future at all.

For many of us, it is a startling reminder. The future—our future—is not unlimited. Each of us is going to run out of time. With regard to the future, we have three choices. We can guess, figure the odds, or trust. Guesses are just that, stabs in the dark. Figuring the odds often works for large populations, but it is almost completely irrelevant for individuals. Hope and trust really are the only two postures that make sense when we think about our relationship to the future.

The future is out of our hands, and so is the past. Each moment that passes is gone for good. There is no getting it back. If the losses, failures, disappointments, and damage are going to be redeemed, it is up to God. We do not have the power to redeem it; God alone is able.

Wednesday's child is full of woe.

It means that the only time we can do anything with or about—the only time we really have—is now. Perhaps real prudence involves being more attentive to how we spend our "nows" rather than what we do with our money. IRAs and 401(k)s? Sure, in moderation. Perhaps even a life of active investing and hedging our bets so long as it brings us pleasure, but there are two things we can be completely certain of. The first is that this day is one day closer than yesterday to our last day on earth, and the second is that the monetary wealth we have accumulated will do us no good whatsoever on the other side of the grave.

> *Gracious God, give us a sense of perspective.*
> *Root us and ground us in the reality of time so that*
> *as much as possible we honor the past and future*
> *but live gladly and gratefully in now. Amen.*

Thursday's child has far to go. **Thursday** ☺

Cheap Eats

Isaiah 55:1 – 2

Hurry! Hurry! Step right up. Right this way, ladies and gentlemen. Here is food that makes you hungry and drink that causes thirst. Clogs your arteries and elevates your blood pressure. Full of salt, fat, and empty calories. Right this way!

Who would accept such an invitation? No one of course, but when the pitch is "Special offer" or "Seventy-five cents off," the response is enthusiastic. The Sunday paper is crammed with coupons pushing empty calories and feel-good fats and sugars. Advertisers know that even lab rats will choose sugar over nutrients and thereby eat themselves to death. Meeting our family's nutritional needs means banishing junk and pursuing value.

Impulse buys are expensive mistakes. Merchants count on us to make them. Where are the real bargains for good, wholesome, nutritious food? Waiting in the grocery store; we just need to find them. Before entering the store, we need to decide

Thursday's child has far to go.

on the foods appropriate for our families and then buy only those. We can't let coupons dictate our purchases.

There are many ways to shop economically. We can check fliers to see what's "in season" (the term applies to more than fruits and vegetables). We can remember to shop with a list and buy in quantity. What we do not use right away we can divide and store. It's perfectly okay to buy sale items but only if they are nutritious.

You can almost always make it tastier, more nutritious, and more cheaply by cooking from scratch. It means keeping staples on hand. An added benefit is the avoidance of preservatives, and we want to avoid buying items that offer only convenience. Prepared foods often come with problems. Pre-chopped salad greens can be breeding grounds of E. coli bacteria, and instant sauce mixes are laced with preservatives. Why pay for the water of canned soups when with a bit of chopping you can make a tasty, robust soup yourself? A basic cornstarch white sauce is the starting point for many delicious sauces and gravies, at a fraction of the cost of ready-made mixes.

Cooking from scratch is a skill that can be learned. There are really only a few basic necessary principles and techniques. Maybe there's a family member or neighbor who would be happy to help. There is surely a community college or university extension service that offers classes.

Getting serious about economical grocery shopping might mean going to one of the deep discount stores. You'll bag your own groceries and pay to use a shopping cart. The discounter's selection is often limited, but the cash register will show your reward. One grocery store advertises itself as our town's "low

Thursday's child has far to go.

price leader," but a deep discounter's prices are twenty to thirty percent less.

There's no need to get grim about it. Buy a frozen pizza when you want. Have some junk food when your family has a real taste for it. Just don't do it without thinking or because you got tricked by an offer that was too good to be true.

> *Thank you for the taste of good food. Thank you, God, for showing us the difference between junk and value. Help us make good choices, so we might eat and not be hungry, drink and be satisfied. Amen.*

Friday

Friday's child is loving and giving.

A Load of Care

MARK 12:28 – 34

It was a bright, sun-shiny day, warm for June. The woman drove into a space beside the community service agency, halfway between the front and back of the building. She unloaded the two bags of canned goods for the food pantry and locked the car door. Balancing the bags on her hips, she gingerly climbed the front steps. At the top she saw a small sign: "Food Pantry—Enter at Rear of Building." The bags were heavy and awkward, so she was careful as she stepped back down to the sidewalk and turned toward the rear of the building.

Walking on this side of the building, she was at least in the shade. Down the entire length of the building she walked and turned another corner. She heaved a sigh as she saw the arrow and read "Food Pantry." The woman felt a surge of renewed energy. She hurried toward the door. It was locked. A small notice indicated that the pantry was not open. A faint "Oh no" escaped the woman. She was hot, sweaty, and close to tears.

The heat seemed to increase. The woman's hair plastered itself to her forehead. Her dress was already pasted against her

Friday's child is loving and giving.

back. She stood at the corner of the building nearest the parking lot, half-tempted to chuck the entire project. Just put the groceries back into the car and forget about it.

No! People were counting on her. The contributors expected their offerings to be delivered. The hungry expected to find food at the pantry. The bags were damp from her sweat. Some of the cans had begun to tear through the paper. The woman squared her shoulders and shifted her load. She could do it. She started back toward the front.

As she began climbing the steps, a man sprang past her to the door. He took the steps with the agility of a mountain goat leaping up a cliff. The woman staggered under her load, but she felt encouraged by the thought, "Ah, he'll hold the door for me. At least I won't have that struggle." As she made the summit, she realized her error. The door swung shut in her face. The quickly closing gap released its final air-conditioned gasp.

The woman's arms were aching. Rims of cans cut into her flesh. Hard edges jabbed her ribs. She debated whether or not to put down the bags to open the door; but holding on seemed the safer course. Once put down, she might not pick them up again. The goal was too near to give up now.

Juggling with intense concentration, the woman wrestled open the door and slipped inside. She found herself in a dark, empty reception area. Before her, down a brightly lit hall, stood two persons engaged in animated conversation. The woman stood silent, waiting to be acknowledged. The unexpected chill of the air made her shiver. The talkers ignored her. The woman watched as the mountain goat tripped from one office to another. No one spoke to the woman.

Friday's child is loving and giving.

The woman entertained a fantasy. She would simply open her arms and let the cans roll away. The image was so clear she could hear the thunder, bangs, and clunks of impact. When people came running and the crowd gathered, she would exclaim, "If this is how you treat someone who's bringing food, how must you treat those who come needing it!"

An attractive scenario, but impossible. The woman cleared her throat and called, "Excuse me. I have some items for the food pantry. I'm leaving them on the counter." She turned away and was gone before anyone could protest.

The woman descended the steps with head held high, feeling noble and long-suffering, a veritable martyr to Christian charity. I should know. I was that woman. I was convinced I had added several gold stars to my heavenly crown and so preoccupied with trumpeting my virtue I did not notice the sour note of sanctimony. Truly, I had received my reward. I had done my duty, but I still carried the load because I hadn't been bearing Jesus' burden of love and joy.

> *Loving God, save us from self-righteousness.*
> *Teach us to be bearers of your love. Shoulder us*
> *with the yoke of lighthearted joy. Amen.*

Saturday's child works hard for a living. Saturday

Projects for the Mechanically Challenged

1 Thessalonians 4:11

These words are for folks who do not work with their hands. If you are a plumber, carpenter, or automobile mechanic, chances are there is nothing useful for you here. If you are an accountant, teacher, or salesperson, however, welcome home. This is for you. Draw your chair up closer to the fire, and give a listen.

When we bought our house, nearly the first thing we did was to cover the soffit and fascia with vinyl. We wanted a low-maintenance home, and what we wanted to paint was certainly not the part that was the highest in the air. "Low-maintenance," we said, not "no-maintenance." The two-car wooden garage out back, we decided to leave exactly as it was.

You probably already know that one of the most frustrating things about working with people and ideas is how very difficult it is to measure progress. Growing and changing take a long time, but it is more than a time problem. The problem is also that it is so very difficult to assign causes for the changes that come.

Saturday's child works hard for a living.

Take teaching for example. Presumably, students' learning results not only from the teaching they get. Who knows why people learn what and when they do? A student might come back ten years later and say, "You really made a difference in my life," and there may be many differences about which you will never know. Students and the ten lepers that Jesus healed have a lot in common. They often do not return.

But I have that wooden garage out back. I can measure my success when I replace a broken windowpane or paint a wall. When it is time to paint, both the process and the results are very satisfying. Scrape, scrape, brush, brush—within a very brief time I can see that I have done some good. The evidence is there, right before my eyes.

What do you have in your life that is like my garage? Don't think only of big and occasional projects. I have an old bookcase out in that garage that I have been working on for years. I doubt that I will ever finish it because the point has nothing to do with finishing. We already have enough bookshelves. We don't need another one. What I do very much need is that project in the garage. I can go out and work on it whenever I want to, whenever I need some evidence that I can actually make a difference.

Don't be misled by examples of projects involving wood. Plumbing has potential too. Though I usually call a plumber, sometimes I don't. For years I have kept my eye on the drain to my stationary tubs in the basement. Patiently I waited for the lint to gum up the works. I knew unclogging that drain would be my contribution to world betterment.

Sure enough. One day I whipped out my father's snake and slammed it into those pipes. Push, grunt, turn—O! It was very satisfying. Before the afternoon was out, I had one of the fastest

Saturday's child works hard for a living.

running drains in all Milwaukee. It didn't last of course. Lint immediately began to collect and slow the drain. Not to worry. When I need an accomplishment again, I'll whip out my father's snake once more and show the world that I really can, and do, make a difference.

I'm thinking right now of a person who might have read all these words and replied, if only to herself, "I don't get it. What's the point?" The point is that we all have favorite ways of being in the world. Sometimes our favorite ways become straitjackets of bondage rather than avenues of blessing. If we're always living out of our heads, for example, we can be corrected by getting in touch with the physical world. It's not that one is better than the other but rather that both are part of the whole. We become more whole ourselves when we strike out into new territory and do the kind of thing we don't ordinarily do.

*Thank you for the work of our lives, dear God.
Thank you especially for the work that lets us know
we really have made a good difference in your world.
Amen.*

Sunday

*But the child born on the Sabbath day
is bright and blithe and bonny and gay.*

The Gift of Fire

EXODUS 3:1 – 6

Something about an open fire calls to the depths of human spirits. Automatic gas heat and programmable thermostats are all well and good, but there's something in us that is drawn by the presence of flame. Candles make a good beginning for contemplating our relationship with fire. "Praying a candle" can be very moving and even illuminating. If you reread the preceding sentence, you will see there is no preposition. It does not say "praying with a candle." Praying a candle is especially powerful for persons who make too many words—persons like me.

Here's how it works for me. I darken the space and light a candle. Then I attempt to completely empty myself of words. It is very difficult at times. If you're like me, your head is full of words. There is a near-constant "head chatter." Simply seeing the candle flame is for me a path to stillness. It's not magic, and it doesn't always work, but when it does, I rediscover "the other side of prayer," the side of receiving. Ironically, the messages I receive sometimes come in words.

But the child born on the Sabbath day is bright and blithe and bonny and gay.

But sometimes a candle flame is not big enough. I long for ... well, a campfire would be ideal, but we are city people, and we are committed to simplifying our lives, so even a fireplace is stretching things. Fireplaces are expensive to procure and operate. Houses with fireplaces are very often more expensive, and the fireplace chimney is proverbial for wasting energy.

The answer at our house is a chimenea. Chimeneas are portable fireplaces made of clay (sometimes iron). We bought ours from the United Community Center for just over $100. A hundred dollars was a pretty good price for a chimenea in 1999, and choosing to buy it from the United Community Center meant that we were supporting both Third World crafts and a community-based organization that does good work among Hispanic immigrants. A garden center in our neighborhood sells wood "by the trunk load" for $36. Chimeneas might, in fact, be preferable to fireplaces. In addition to the economic advantages, there are more subtle benefits.

When we sit around our chimenea, we are accessible to our neighbors. Neighboring really is almost a lost art in modern USAmerica. Whatever we can do to retrieve it is good for us all. The charm of an open fire attracts people. They slow down, look, and perhaps exchange the news. Sometimes we slip into deeper conversation.

More subtly still, a chimenea is better than a fireplace in exactly the same way that eating fresh local produce is better than buying hothouse tomatoes in January. Tomatoes from one's own garden in September actually taste better, of course, but the superiority is heightened by living in harmony with the natural world.

Although not native to Wisconsin, chimeneas connect us to the natural world in at least two ways. First, they are working

But the child born on the Sabbath day is bright and blithe and bonny and gay.

examples of folk art. Their shape has evolved over centuries so that the wood burns completely and efficiently, and the clay gets hot enough that one can be quite comfortable even on a very cool evening. But, secondly, one does not sit around the chimenea in a January snowstorm or even on the coldest nights in November. Chimenea season ends when the nip in the air turns icy. This hearthside experience is another reminder of our limits and dependence.

For me, praying a candle is refreshing, but praying a chimenea approaches ecstasy. The flames leap, their colors dance from red to blue to gold, the blaze turns to coals, and the wood makes faint metallic chimes as it burns to the last. I get lost in the fire of the chimenea and then go inside enlivened and renewed.

You come too. We'll put the coffee on for you and spend some companionable time around the fire.

Thank you, dear God, for light and heat. Thank you for slowing us down and reminding us that there is nothing better than spending time with you. Amen.

Monday's child is fair of face.   **Monday**

Orthorexia

Psalm 24:1 – 6

Orthorexia is a term so new my spell-checker doesn't recognize it. The computer knows *anorexia* and *bulemia* but not *orthorexia*. This exotic-sounding eating disorder is the constant worry about healthful diet. *Orthodoxy* means "right praise." *Orthorexia* means "right eating." Orthorexics say things like, "I was at a restaurant and saw a family—every one of them was obese—eating fried chicken with mashed potatoes and gravy. Just wallowing in cholesterol!" or, "Oranges should be eaten directly from the tree. If you wait fifteen minutes, the vitamins are virtually gone."

Erica is orthorexic. It is almost painful to lunch with her. There is nothing "fit to eat" on the menu. "I eat only free-range chicken, and no red meat. Ugh!" She quizzes the waitperson about the methods of preparation and the amount of polyunsaturated fat in each item. "You use olive oil? That's good. And is your lettuce organically grown? Not just iceberg, either?" When the orders come, she eyes your plate with distaste and giving a small but perceptible shudder begins eating.

Monday's child is fair of face.

Food isn't the only concern of the orthorexic. Drink too is suspect, even if it's only water. Erica drinks only bottled water. "Have you read what's in that vile liquid that comes from the tap? Ugh!" The irony is that though the water system is subject to close scrutiny and chemical testing, bottled water is not. I haven't tried to tell Erica; I doubt she would believe me.

Now that there are "enhanced" bottled waters on the market, I expect to see Erica sipping one any day. Given her aversion to soft drinks, she's a likely consumer even though they are more expensive than her regular brand. Unfortunately, the enhanced bottled waters are actually fortified only with sweeteners and contain minuscule amounts of vitamins and minerals.

Erica shops exclusively at health-food stores, Eden for orthorexics. The groceries there cost about four times as much as at a regular supermarket, but Erica asserts, "When it's your health, you can't fool around." Health-food stores locate in high-income areas. Poor folks can't afford health-food stores.

Eating a healthful diet is part of good stewardship. Orthorexia, however, worships at an idol's shrine. Actually, orthorexics care neither about calories nor even cookery but only control.

They are consumed by their food consumption. It is dietary luxury that can be indulged only in an affluent society. A starving person doesn't ask, "Is this bread made with stone ground, unbleached, whole grain flour?" Orthorexia makes a "god of the belly" as surely as gluttony.

Oh, Erica, how I understand your need for control. I too need to feel I'm running things. I'm not in control of anything, not even myself. The best I can do is take responsibility and then trust God to make up the difference.

Monday's child is fair of face.

Orthorexics can twist anything, even Scripture, to fit their obsession. Consider the story of "The Miracle of the Loaves and Fishes," NOV (New Orthorexic Version). The disciple comes to offer fish and bread. Orthorexic Erica replies, "I'll pass on the fish. It looks smoked. Too many carcinogens! Ugh. I'll just have the bread, thanks—if it's made with sprouted barley." The disciple's eyebrows raise in astonishment.

Erica, I cringe inside when I hear you talk like this. Maybe that's why I'm so hard on you. You remind me of my own grasping at control. We're afraid of grace, Erica. God invites us to a party, but we don't feel worthy of the invitation until we believe we've paid for our ticket. We can't, won't, and never will.

The disciple moves on, and Erica leans toward a neighbor, "Fish is very good for you—filled with omega oils—but not if it's smoked." While everyone else sits stunned by abundance, Erica picks at her food. "Actually," she says, " I would prefer a whole grain muffin—with maybe a dab of honey, and no butter."

> *Merciful God, forgive us for all the ways we exert inappropriate control. We ask for grace to trust your authority over our lives. Help us surrender fully to you and your love. Amen.*

Tuesday

Tuesday's child is full of grace.

I've Got a Home in Glory Land That Outshines the Sun

1 CORINTHIANS 15:51–57

Every first Sunday of the month the Broken Walls Christian Community worships at the Jackson Center, a residential treatment center for persons who happen to be mentally challenged. Worship is designed for a minimum of words and intellectualizing and a maximum of emotion, movement, and touch.

Although worship was designed precisely for her strengths and weaknesses, Judy wasn't having any. She would either come to worship late or sit out in the kitchen with a cup of coffee waiting for worship to end. Ah, but when worship did end, Judy came alive. She would hurry down to me as fast as she could move, grab my hands, and begin a spirited singing and dancing of "Do Lord."

The rest of the folks in the room pretty much ignored us. The worshiping congregation at the Jackson Center is quite tolerant of differing abilities and desires. Sometimes, however, Judy and I were having so much obvious fun that others would want to join in.

Tuesday's child is full of grace.

Judy had Down's syndrome and was in her mid-fifties. As is often the case for folks with Down's syndrome at this stage of life, Judy's deterioration recently had been dramatic. One day in March, the year of grace 2002, Judy was taking a bath without an attendant present. She slipped into the water and drowned.

Easter Sunday morning at the Jackson Center was a celebration of resurrection indeed. It began with a surprise. Before the "warm-up singing," a woman in a wheelchair (a new resident or perhaps merely someone who had not come to worship before) started singing "He'll Carry You Through." It is one of the favorite old hymns of some parts of the African-American Church:

> *Ask the Savior to help you.*
> *He'll comfort and guide you.*
> *He is able to save you.*
> *He'll carry you through.*

Folks at the Jackson Center don't always stop and pay attention to each other, but they did this time. The room hushed, and the second time through the chorus Mabel was joined by others, and some, who could not manage words, rocked to the rhythm.

I don't know how many of us were thinking about Judy, but I know I was not alone. At prayer time, someone said, "Do you know about Judy, David? She died." Someone else added, "She's in heaven with Jesus now." Yet a third person said, "Why don't we sing 'Do Lord' for them? I'll bet they'd like that."

So we did—right then in prayer time, softly and reverently as a beginning to prayer and then, at the end of the service, as boisterously as could be. We paired up, some of us standing,

Tuesday's child is full of grace.

some in wheelchairs. We joined hands as Judy and I used to do, and those of the thirty-six of us who could make words caroled,

> *Do Lord,*
> *Oh, do Lord,*
> *Oh, do remember me.*
> *Look away beyond the blue.*

> *Thank you, Lord Jesus, for all the folks you have given us to love and be loved by. Thank you that we are learning to look at each other with your eyes and see the beloved of God. Amen.*

Wednesday's child is full of woe.   **Wednesday** 🙂

Internal Fireworks

PSALM 90:9–12

Fear is a wonderful concentrator of attention.

The first time I saw the flashing lights arranging themselves in a grid-pattern, I thought, "Is this what it's like at the beginning of a stroke?" and went immediately to my recliner and became very still. Soon the flashing lights went away. Both arms worked, both legs. I experimented with talking and discovered that I could.

So if not a stroke, I said to myself, perhaps a detaching retina or at least some kind of trouble with my eyes. A brief phone conversation with my optometrist confirmed my hunch that this was an experience worth taking seriously. An ophthalmologist cleared space for me later that afternoon, another confirmation that we were dealing with a potentially major event, and Lo-Ann was soon driving me to the doctor.

How frustrated I was with that obtuse young man! He kept asking me the same questions over and over and didn't seem able to get my answers straight. He continued misstating what I told

Wednesday's child is full of woe.

him, and finally I got exasperated. "Now listen to me," I said. "You've got the order wrong. Here's what happened."

He gave himself away by the little smile that flitted across his face. It was there for only the briefest moment, but the light dawned. He's not obtuse. In fact, he is quite clever. He knows very well what I've been saying. His "misunderstanding" and "getting it wrong" are ways of checking my memory and mental acuity. This is how he determines whether I have had a stroke.

Dr. Gordon saw that the light had dawned for me, and we both relaxed and started a more truly mutual conversation. Without blood work he wasn't willing to be "absolutely sure, but I think you suffered the beginning of a migraine."

Fear is a wonderful concentrator of attention, and relief is a powerful impetus to distraction. I left the doctor, went home, and over the next few years practiced recognition of an incipient migraine, then practiced the behaviors that would nip it in the bud long before the full-fledged pain.

But I got careless, and lazy. One evening while doing the laundry, I noticed the slight flicker of lights but said to myself, "Not yet. It's early. You've got time. Just finish this load, and then you can take care of it."

Big mistake. By the time I got to my chair, the lights were intense, the flashing was strobe-like, and the pain had begun. Not even closing my eyes, breathing deeply, and beginning to meditate did any good. The lights kept flashing, and the pain grew. The fireworks were memorable; but it is a show I do not want to see again.

Wednesday's child is full of woe.

> *Thank you, God, for all the reminders of our mortality. Thank you that each moment is so very precious precisely because the moments are so limited. Teach us to number our days and pay attention, so that we live gladly and gratefully in your blessings. Amen.*

Thursday

Thursday's child has far to go.

Shop 'Til You Drop

AMOS 2:6 – 8

Do you know the Wordsworth sonnet that begins,

The world is too much with us; late and soon,
Getting and spending, we soon lay waste our powers;
Little we see in nature that is ours;
We have given our hearts away: a sordid boon!

How did Wordsworth know that shopping malls were coming? Getting and spending, indeed! Not only is there little we see in nature that is ours, but we are able to purchase only a minute portion of all we see in the stores. For what? So we can hoard it like misers? So we can be surrounded by more toys than we have time, energy, or desire to play with?

When I teach this poem to college freshmen, they usually have a hard time getting it. Some never do. Most of my students are poor, but even the more affluent ones, perhaps especially they, are so immersed in getting and spending that the only downside they can see is the need to get more so they can spend more in order to get more, which is exactly what Wordsworth says is so wrong.

Thursday's child has far to go.

Is it wrong to love shopping so much? If so, why? As an acquaintance said recently, "I don't see why I should be bothered by wanting to have nice things. Don't I deserve them? After all, I worked hard for what I have, and lots of people have more than I do. Why should I be ashamed?"

The answer is that we shall never be able to buy enough to free us from our shame. Shame and guilt are not the same. Guilt is the awareness of doing something wrong (or not doing something right). Shame is the sense of *being* wrong—not worth it, not good enough, having no right even to be alive. We are not all equally aware of our shame, of course, but we are all equally in need of the great good news that God loves us as we are.

Shame is the deep sickness that needs to be healed, and it is impossible to buy our way out of feeling worthless. If buying were the cure, sooner or later we would have peace. We would reach a point at which we had accumulated enough.

How much is enough? Twenty pairs of shoes? Thirty? More? A new $38,000 car to replace the one that had 50,000 miles on it and was running just fine? Compulsively buying each new software bell and whistle as soon as it comes out? Rowboat, motorboat, cabin cruiser, yacht. Shopping for happiness and contentment is a hopeless task with a huge price tag.

The point of "enough" never arrives because what we are shopping for cannot be bought. Our getting and spending are just like the hamster on its wheel: frantic flying of legs, round and round, going nowhere.

I overheard some students talking a couple of semesters ago. They were supposed to be discussing their writing project, but they had gotten distracted and didn't know I was listening.

"What did you do last weekend?" one of them asked.

Thursday's child has far to go.

"Went wish shopping."

"Wish shopping. What's that?"

"Well, it's like when you don't have any money, you know, and you're not gonna have any, but there are all these pretty things. So you walk and look, and when you see something that you would really like, you stop and wish real hard."

Wish shopping! Whether or not we have any money. Trying to get and spend our way to happiness is pursuing phantoms. When we get our wish, we still won't have what we really want, because what we want isn't tangible.

The only way to stop the whirling hamster wheel is to let God reclaim the hearts we have set on the stores' well-stocked shelves. Our shame has caused us to pursue material "treasures" in place of God's free gift. Only when we really accept God's announcement, "You are precious, worthy, and bought at great price," will we be able to say, "This is what I really want and truly need."

> *Thank you, God, that this world is not only things; that the best things are, indeed, free. Thank you that love, hope, joy, and the rest of the blessings have almost nothing to do with coins. Amen.*

Friday's child is loving and giving. **Friday**

Neither a Borrower Nor . . .

LUKE 6:35 – 36

Folk wisdom says, "Never lend money to family or friends." We're mixed about that wisdom because of our experience.

In January 1993, a significant chunk of money dropped into our lives. We needed to find out what to do with it, so we ran some experiments. We have changed all the names of the subjects of these experiments and some of the identifying details.

We asked ourselves, "Where can this money do the most good?" and quickly decided that at least some of it would be well invested in the lives of others. We knew some teenagers and young adults who were establishing themselves, financially and otherwise, who had not yet acquired credit ratings. They therefore would have a hard time obtaining conventional loans. We let it be known that we had some money available for appropriate projects.

Given our target audience, it is not surprising that the purchase of cars topped the list. Three of our young borrowers intended to buy cars. Two of the three repaid their loans in a

Friday's child is loving and giving.

timely fashion, and then there was Clarence. Clarence wanted $1,000, but he didn't have a very trustworthy track record, so we told him his limit was $500. Clarence wanted to buy a car so he could get a job in an industrial park beyond the bus line.

He did get his car, but we never got our money. Not a penny. Clarence didn't make even his first payment.

Another borrower—let's call him Sam—was slightly older. We loaned him $1,000 to repair his house. He agreed to pay back the loan at the rate of $100 a month.

Sam's first payment was two months late. "But don't worry," he said. "After all, you're still making money on the interest."

Sam's loan should have been paid off within a year. Almost three years later, Sam's balance still stood at $100.94. The largest payment he ever made was $70, but more usually it was $20 or $30. He occasionally skipped a month, but he eventually did discharge his debt. We made nine loans to people who could really use the money. Six of them repaid on time; one returned the check without ever cashing it, and Sam was late. And then there is Clarence. What did we learn?

The most important thing is that people deal with money just as they deal with the rest of their lives. If they are responsible with time, they tend to be responsible with money. If their word can be trusted about what they witnessed, their word is also probably good when it comes to financial transactions.

Equally important is our reaffirmation that people are more important than money.

We are no longer in relationship with two of our nine clients. That lack of connection, as far as we know, has nothing to do with the loans. Clarence, however, paid a price for his betrayal even though he never paid back the money. His loan was made

Friday's child is loving and giving.

in June of 1993, and then he dropped out of sight. The last time he called was late in 1995—to ask for another favor.

If he calls again, what should we say?

> *Help us, God, use our money and our lives in ways that honor you. Grant us the mercy to be merciful to others, and help us to recognize and meet genuine need. Amen.*

Saturday

Saturday's child works hard for a living.

Get a(nother) Job!

ISAIAH 65:17–25

One of the reasons we've been able to thrive—that is, live joyously—without ever making much money is that we have always been willing to take weird jobs. I drove a cab, off and on, from when I was first in college (1961) until I graduated seminary (1977), and I would be willing to do it again if that were where life leads. Lo-Ann tells stories and plays music for occasional cash. Once she catered private parties.

The jobs we held in the first six months of one year include artistic director of an amateur theatre company, drama teacher, music teacher, professional musician, storyteller, freelance writer, writing teacher, pastor, and now we are writing another book. What fun, and what an invitation to live in a bigger and more interesting world.

What matters most about our jobs is not the money but the experiences themselves. I am thinking now of 1980. We were both unemployed and barely scraping by, and the summer was upon us. I said to myself, "Summer equals hot. Hot equals ice

Saturday's child works hard for a living.

cream. I'll bet I could make some quick money selling ice cream on the streets of Milwaukee."

It was an amazing experience that did not last very long. My fair skin quickly burned and blistered despite my wide-brimmed straw hat and long-sleeved shirt. The end of the experience was taking my employer to small claims court (we settled before the case came to trial), but the most important part of the experience for me was the article I wrote and sold to *Lutheran Forum* (writing is not a full-time job for us, but it does pay some of the mortgage, and writers always keep their eyes open for story possibilities and money-making opportunities). That article is titled "Nothing Personal, You Understand."

Little did I know back in the summer of 1980 that I was driving my motorized ice cream tricycle through exactly the same neighborhood where, six years later, we were to buy our house. I remember, despite the rigors of the job and the difficulty of selling very much ice cream, how much I was attracted to the community, and I even remember driving into Smith Park (which is a half block south of the home we later purchased) and ringing my bells.

Although the experience was personally painful, I learned a lot. One thing I learned is that many folks don't have nearly as many choices as I. One morning, for example, a young man tried to join our company, but he didn't have the required $50 deposit. Another day I learned of the woman whose bike had broken down early in the morning. She stayed with it all day and made a profit of only pennies from her long toil in the sun. A good number of my colleagues were robbed and a few of them injured.

I also learned some things about this city we now live in. Too many children are left too long unsupervised. Consequently, they

Saturday's child works hard for a living.

get into trouble and never develop the skills and attitudes necessary for success in postmodern culture. These are not very pleasant lessons, but they have helped me ever since to look at the world more with Jesus' eyes. There is blessing and pleasure aplenty, to be sure, but there is sadness and desperation and need. I wouldn't have known it quite as I do without those terrible days of trying to sell ice cream.

So let's end with a suggestion. What part of the world would you like to explore next? What job would test your desire, increase your knowledge base, and promote your spiritual maturity? Part-time, of course. Neither of us has had a full-time job for more than twenty years, and we earnestly commend to you the freedom and joy of that condition.

Are you happy at work? Are you doing what you want and were meant to do? How might you expand your personal horizons by going out and getting a(nother) job?

> *Thank you for the joy of work, great God. Thank you for the pleasure, satisfaction, and all the wonderful learnings. Teach us to seek and work diligently at the jobs you have for us. Amen.*

*But the child born on the Sabbath day
is bright and blithe and bonny and gay.*

Sunday

You Deserve a Break Today

EXODUS 20:8–11

The goodness of idleness is much undervalued. Remember, even God took a day off!

I'm not talking about a life of indolence. That is quite a different thing. The wasted life with no productivity and no passion is a sign of sickness and sin. When whole lives are characterized by low energy, it means that something significant has gone wrong. It means, most often, that a wound got covered over without ever having healed.

The idleness that deserves celebrating is the rest that comes after hard struggle for a goal that really matters. The rest is merited whether or not the goal has been achieved. The rest is a constituent part of the activity and is as important and valuable as the disciplined expenditure of energy.

One of the wisest things my friend Robert ever said to me was, "I'm willing to work like crazy over the summer if I can have the winter for the other things that matter." Robert was a man of very limited means. He had been poorly educated and not only in terms of school. He didn't have many marketable

But the child born on the Sabbath day is bright and blithe and bonny and gay.

skills, but he was strong, energetic, and teachable. The important things he wanted to do in the winter included spending time with family and friends, working in his church, and just plain woolgathering.

Me too. I have been more fortunate than Robert in my education. I don't have to buy a winter's meaning with a frantic summer. Like Robert, though, I love times of idleness without the need to do anything, just being if I choose.

I confess that woolgathering is one of my favorite things. Sometimes I turn the wool I gather into threads to weave into poems. Other times, I just let the wool lie there until it joins the dust bunnies under the bed and hibernates until spring.

How about you? Have you become completely addicted to a life of doing, or are you willing—even eager—to let it go sometimes and just experience this magnificent creation? It really is magnificent, you know. There are miracles and mysteries all around. We often forget that. We live with our noses so pressed to the grindstone that we forget—or never discover—what we are here for.

What's that? You don't know what we're here for? The purpose of our existence, I am most extremely happy to tell you, is to love and enjoy God forever. Whatever furthers that purpose is, to that very extent, good. Whatever does not further that purpose must be—however reluctantly—let go. One of these good things is pleasurable idleness. You do deserve a break today—maybe more than one. Take it as gladly and gratefully as you can, and then try to remember to share the joy.

But the child born on the Sabbath day is bright and blithe and bonny and gay.

> *Thank you for rest, dear God. Teach us to be just like you: active and alive, living at full power, creating beauty and meaning; then settling in for a time of sitting quietly and just being gratefully in your world. Amen.*

Monday

Monday's child is fair of face.

Toss It Out!

Luke 12:39–40

There is a thief in your house—probably more than one. This criminal is stealing your time, energy, attention; indeed, your very being. The thief is your television, and it's time for the TV to go.

There is one exception. If someone living in your home is so utterly incapacitated that they need it, let them keep their television, but be sure to restrict viewing to that infirm one. Even under these circumstances, your ultimate goal may well be to get rid of the television, but you can delay tossing it out until you make other plans.

We tossed our television in 1979. Actually, we gave it to a church rummage sale. If we had known then what we know now, we would have hit that television over the head with a sledgehammer rather than inflicting it upon anyone else. But time has passed, and that black and white portable is surely long dead.

Television is more than not good for us. It is positively evil. TV induces physical and intellectual passivity and encourages emotional isolation. It distracts from the important things in life,

Monday's child is fair of face.

and the little bit of good it accomplishes is done much more powerfully in other ways.

TV promotes physical passivity. Couch potatoes indeed! Is there anything more indolent than potentially vital, exuberant, alive children sprawled on the floor in front of the television? Yes, there is. The more indolent thing is their parents slouched on the couch, in a semiconscious state of stupefaction. The physical condition mirrors the intellectual. Images from the television come too quickly to be really attended, much less reflected upon. There is no time to engage the images, to discriminate among them, or to evaluate what they mean. Real life is communication. Real communication is always two- (or more-than-two-) way.

TV also encourages emotional isolation. Even if the television room is packed with people, each one is usually quite completely alone. The child says, "Watch me, Daddy. See this," and the father replies, "Not now, Kristen. Can't you see that I'm watching television?"

Physical, intellectual, and emotional damage—that about covers it. Could there be anything else wrong with television? Yes, there could.

TV distracts us from more important things. TV distracts us not only from our children but from everyone else in the room. Surely, persons are much more important than television, but even if you're alone, you are distracted—from yourself. If you were to turn off the television (better yet, toss it out) and pay attention to what is going on inside you, you would discover that you are infinitely more interesting than television. You might not make that discovery right away. It might take a little time and energy to arrive at that learning, but you are worth that time and

Monday's child is fair of face.

energy. Give yourself, rather than your television, your energy and time.

The good TV does is accomplishable much more effectively and efficiently in a host of other ways. What good is that? Education? Read a book, or run an experiment. Entertainment? Read a book, or play a game. Relaxation? Read a book, or take the nap you have long been needing. Distraction from your problems? Read a book, or face your problems head-on. Baby sitting? Bad idea! TV turns children into zombies whose heads are being filled with sour cottage cheese.

Most of us watch television when we feel lazy, tired, or scared. TV confirms our laziness, further wearies us, and only momentarily distracts us from our fears.

Toss it out—if you have the courage. At bare minimum, take it out to the garage or down to the basement, and then declare that area quarantined. If nothing else, you can keep the disease isolated until you find courage for the cure.

*Thank you, God, for the real stuff of life. Thank you that we do not have to settle for pale imitations.
Amen.*

Tuesday's child is full of grace. **Tuesday**

Angels Among Us

1 JOHN 4:17–21

She sits at the end of your pew, a tall attractive woman, stylishly dressed, with steel gray hair. If you look very closely, you might notice that her right earlobe is split—the only external clue to "the best thing that ever happened."

Her name is Amy. She has a story to tell, but she's "not one for many words." She's a doer, not a talker. She once opened her home to a teenager needing refuge from a dangerous, drug-ridden lifestyle. She recently has been the guardian angel of a testy elderly aunt who lives alone. You'll recognize her at church—she's the one who cleans the refrigerator.

Her life was never easy. Her mother married, young, a domineering man. That marriage went sour, and the young wife found another man. The coy, flirtatious mother pursued male attention while the children were left in the care of their father. She wanted—needed—male attention.

It's time for your bath.

But, Mama, please. I don't want to.

Tuesday's child is full of grace.

Oh, Amy, don't start complaining. I'm going—out. I don't have time for any of your arguments.

Mama, please. He puts his fingers—

I'm not going to listen to any more of your excuses. Your father is waiting to give you your bath. Go.

Amy was alone with her father when he had his fatal heart attack. He simply turned blue and collapsed. She was fourteen and didn't know what to do. Her guilt and anger drove her to elope the next year. Soon there were children.

I don't get it, Amy. What's with you and the God thing? You always make us—me and the kids—go with you to church every Sunday. Why? I can see that it matters to you, but why can't I feel it too?

I don't know how to explain it, Eddie. It's just something I've felt since I was a little girl. This closeness to God. When I was little somebody gave me a New Testament. I treasured it and read it. I guess I've always felt close to God.

Then Amy was diagnosed with cancer. The treatment at the time was radical double mastectomy, even to the extent of removing some muscle from the chest wall. It was a long, painful, and difficult recovery. After twenty-two years of marriage, it led to divorce.

You're a freak. I don't want to be married to you anymore. I don't want you. Nobody else is gonna want you either.

Not only did Eddie leave her with three children to raise on her own; he emptied their bank account, forged her name to their insurance policies, and cashed them in. Amy was left alone without resources. Yet when Eddie was dying and asking to see her, she forgave him. "Some people just can't take it," Amy says. "Eddie didn't have any faith to help him through. I couldn't not forgive him. He was dying."

Tuesday's child is full of grace.

Amy bounced back. She returned to school, got her GED, and started working. Eventually, she and a friend started their own interior decorating business. Life was going smoothly. Then her world imploded—again.

Amy's mother was diagnosed with terminal cancer. Amy took her mother in to care for her. At about the same time, Amy's breast implants began causing problems. Within the next few months, she lost all her assets when her business partner went through an ugly divorce. The devastating combination sent Amy into depression. She sought solace in alcohol. God seemed very far away, but gradually the darkness lifted. Amy was able to say, "I love my children. Money isn't important to me. My life has been good. God has blessed me."

While the team assembles, the emergency room nurse cuts the clothes from the "Code Blue" the paramedics just brought in. She reaches over and pulls the earring from the patient's right ear. It is a pierced earring. The patient begins bleeding, but no one notices because the situation is so critical.

The doctors and nurses gather. Their urgency is palpable. High above them the woman floats serene. She sees her body lying on the table. She sees the medical team working frantically to revive her. Suffusing her being is a sense of warmth and love. In the ear of her ears she hears, "I give you this gift because in your life you have so rarely felt loved."

It is the best thing that ever happened to her.

> *Loving God, when everything seems hopeless and we are in despair, fill us with your Spirit. When we feel unloved, unlovely, and unlovable, embrace us in the everlasting arms of your eternal care. Amen.*

Wednesday

Wednesday's child is full of woe.

Fore!

Hebrews 3:12–14

Golf and I are not great friends. Our common history is filled with a long string of disappointments. My first sin against golf was that I took it up for all the wrong reasons. I was a working class boy who very much wanted to rise, and I hoped golf would help me. As far as I know, it never did, but I may not be being fair. Had I ever played golf for the sheer fun of it, who knows what might have happened?

Just before the death of my father, golf and I had another bad experience. Dad's terminal cancer had just been diagnosed, and he said it was time for him to do something he had long wanted to do. "Just drive from golf course to golf course," Dad said, "and play the ones you want to. No specific schedule and no particular direction. When you're done with a course, drive to the next one that attracts you, wherever that might be, and play another round. Keep it up," Dad said, "as long as you want to. Until you're done."

So we did.

Wednesday's child is full of woe.

I was resolved to have the experience in exactly the way Dad wanted and to keep on sharing it with him until he was through. It was a disaster. Dad played terrible golf and was furiously angry most of the time. Nothing went right on or off the golf course. I heard more profanity from my father's mouth in those ten days than in all of the rest of the time that I knew him. It was a disaster, or at least I thought so until Dad's visitation. Dad's old buddies from work sought me out, inquired if I were the son he had golfed with, and after hearing that I was, said things like ...

"Wasn't that a wonderful time!"

"Harold could never stop talking about it. You must have really had fun."

"After your father told me that story, I resolved to get closer to my own kids."

These comments were not all made at the same time, you understand. They came from different men at separate meetings, and now, fifteen years later, I still do not understand them. My golf clubs are down in the basement now. I haven't had them out for years. I really couldn't tell you why I never sold them or just gave them away.

The reason golf is back on my mind is that my eldest son, Matthew, called me three Saturdays ago. He was angry—not an auspicious sign. The upshot of it is that we have two days of golf scheduled. I suspect that I shall be happy with whatever bogeys I manage. Pars or better would be a taste of paradise, I think, but I wonder why we have to go golfing. Wouldn't we all be much better off if we just took a walk?

When Matthew comes to my visitation, what sorts of tales will my old buddies tell?

Wednesday's child is full of woe.

{ *Thank you for the fun of life, dear God. Help us not to treat our play like work unless we're having so much fun that it doesn't make any difference. Amen.* }

Thursday's child has far to go.

Thursday

Turning a Prophet

Ephesians 4:11–13

We are sitting in the monthly business meeting of the congregation. The facilities committee has just reported that another group would like to use the building. Ms. Pierce, chair of finance, is the first to speak. "We have a number of outside groups using our church for meetings. They need to pay their way. After all, we have to pay the janitor and the utility bills. We can't go on carrying these outsiders. I say, no more free rides!"

"That's right," comments the president. "And don't forget all these different groups make for wear and tear on the building too. Just last week the Tuesday night Twelve-Steppers left a window open on the first floor. The police called me at midnight to come over. They thought we had a break in. I had to make sure nothing had been stolen."

"And there's the mess," contributed Ms. Hines, housekeeping and hospitality chair. "All the tracking in and out. There are scuff marks in the west hall, fingerprints all over the furniture in the parlor, and we can't keep paper towels in all the dispensers."

Thursday's child has far to go.

"We'll just have to raise the rates for building use," asserts Ms. Pierce. "Anything else is not sound business practice. We'll let them use our facilities, but we should be making a little money out of this as well."

"Hey!" exclaims another member. "I was just talking to somebody over at Covenant. They're renting to the Boys and Girls Club. Those groups get grant money. They have big bucks. That's who we should rent to."

"Good idea."

More and more segments of our society are adopting the business model. Altruism and social responsibility are being judged according to cost-benefit analysis in medicine, education, and even the church. Doctors learn to perform certain surgical procedures such as laser vision correction because it is quick, easy, and profitable. Physicians are cashing in on the USAmerican obsession with weight loss by selling prepackaged diet programs and foods. Gone are the days when Old Doc Henderson was willing to make a house call because your lumbago was kicking up. Medicine is big, big business.

Education too, once the cornerstone of enlightened democratic process, has succumbed to the lures of business. Education has become training, outcomes are measured, and performance is evaluated. Student retention now means not what students learn and remember but rather keeping enrollments high in order to generate more tuition dollars. These trends conflict with USAmerican historical precedent. Public education began in the Sunday schools of New England. Poor children were taught to read by studying the Bible. Education was an act of mission and service. Now, however, education is business.

Thursday's child has far to go.

Just like Ms. Pierce and her colleagues in their business meeting, the church too has begun making choices based on the bottom line. Churches have focus groups and consult demographics to cater to particularly desirable clienteles. They purchase promotional packages to market their image and hire consultants to develop new programming.

The church is intended to be Christ's body in the world, continuing his ministry and mission. In his life on earth Jesus said of himself, "Foxes have holes and birds have nests but the Son of Man has nowhere to lay his head." The clincher of his parable about a rich person who wanted to expand his profits and secure his future is, "This night your soul will be required of you." Jesus teaches there is a conflict of interest when it comes to serving God or serving money. "No one can serve two masters. You will be devoted to one and despise the other."

When Jesus commissioned the first disciples, he told them to proclaim good news, cure the sick, cleanse the unclean, cast out evil. Specifically, he admonished, "You received without paying; give without payment" (see Matthew 10:5–15; Luke 10:4–12). We must decide whether these words apply equally also to modern disciples like you and me.

The president of the congregation has concluded the discussion. "All those in favor of the motion, signify by saying 'Aye.'"

How will you vote?

Thank you, God, that you give us so much freedom to make choices. Help us discover and claim our ministries. Build up your church to a measure of the stature of Christ, in whose name we serve. Amen.

Friday

Friday's child is loving and giving.

Famous Lost Words

ROMANS 8:12–17

While shopping I stopped at the testers on the cosmetics counter. I wanted to savor the fragrance of my favorite cologne. Spritz! Ah! Smile. The clerk approached and asked, "Can I help you?"

"No, not really. I yielded to temptation and took a detour to your department."

"Would you care to see anything in this line?"

"No, thanks. This is my favorite scent, but I'm not buying anything for myself. I'm shopping for a birthday present."

There was a pause and the clerk turned away; but before she withdrew, she said, "Well, don't deny yourself."

Though her words didn't make me stop and buy at her counter, they did have lasting effect. I found them unexpectedly coming back to me and caught myself ruminating on them. They disturbed me in peculiar and elusive ways.

Don't deny yourself. The cologne was expensive. The clerk seemed to deliver an affirming message, saying that I deserved to pamper myself with this little luxury. I deserved to feel good.

Friday's child is loving and giving.

By not buying her cologne I was, she implied, undervaluing myself. Her affirmation was compromised, however, by its connection to a sales commission. No, I needed to look further.

Don't deny yourself. I pondered whether or not I had been paying attention to my inner life. I took inventory. I was keeping current in my journal, my prayer life was rich and satisfying, and I didn't feel deprived of affection or attention. What's more, my spouse and colleagues were appreciative of my efforts at home and work. Nothing seemed lacking. I didn't believe I was denying myself, yet the words still echoed in my head.

Don't deny yourself. I entertained another alternative. Perhaps I had been compromising my values in some way. If anything, I felt a certain pride that I had objected during a meeting to a policy change that could have had disturbing consequences. Raising my misgivings allowed others to voice theirs, and the measure failed for lack of support. No, I had been true to my core beliefs.

Don't deny yourself. I had been saving my money for the present. I could blow it on the cologne and then buy a less expensive gift with what was left over. That choice, however, would be denying myself too. I had anticipated the surprise and delight of the recipient. I knew they would welcome and enjoy the intended present. My momentary pleasure in purchasing the cologne could not compete with the multifaceted satisfaction of a gift well bestowed.

Ah, I finally realized why the words were familiar. I recognized their source, though slightly modified from their original. Jesus had said them first. Only he said, "Deny yourself. Take up your cross and follow me."

The clerk's words were intended as a prod to self-indulgence. As I focused on me and my needs, I ought to have been increasingly

Friday's child is loving and giving.

gratified, but I wasn't. It was not until I started thinking beyond myself that I got a clue to Jesus' meaning, and I think I'm right.

When we are living centered lives and know we have what we need, we can begin looking outward toward others. It is when we recognize our giftedness and know we are blessed that we want to become a blessing to others. It sounds paradoxical: Denying ourselves can mean affirming who we truly are. When we deny our puny, self-serving desires, we connect with God's bigger reality. Our truest reality is becoming part of Christ. Martin Luther said we were to "be Christ" to others. We find out who we were meant to be when we deny the lesser self we are.

> *Thank you, good God, for Jesus' self-giving love.*
> *May we empty ourselves in order to be filled*
> *with your grace. Help us lose ourselves in you,*
> *so that we can truly find ourselves. Amen.*

Saturday's child works hard for a living. Saturday

Luddites need not Apply

 EZRA 3:10–11

Technology is certainly not the savior of humankind, but neither is it necessarily the enemy. Many folks who are interested in simplifying life bewail our increased reliance on technology and mechanization, but consider the blessings of modern times. Water and sewers, electricity at the flip of a switch, food in abundance, antibiotics—it is a long list of blessings, and these are only the barest beginning.

I began my writing career in 1970, on a Royal standard office typewriter. Many thousand pages passed around that roller and under those keys, and when computers came, I was most reluctant to change. Praise God for colleagues! Mine kept harping on the need to get current until I finally took the plunge and purchased a Smith Corona Personal Word Processor. The first time I moved text felt like a miracle. In the old days, a mistake on page one meant either correction fluid (if the job was not very "important") or retyping the entire manuscript. But now it was a matter of a few strokes of the keys, and the words move around as if by magic.

Saturday's child works hard for a living.

A common writer's problem is to write one's way into the subject, thereby having material at the beginning that must be deleted. The word processor made the task a snap. I have often wondered where all those words go when they are deleted. Cyberspace, I know, but what does that mean? All those words flying around hoping to find where they belong!

Smith Corona Personal Word Processors were never meant for professional writers. The drive wore out before the first year was over, so I moved up to a used IBM computer. I don't remember the name of it, but it used five-and-a-quarter-inch floppies, so some of you with good memories will know what I mean. DOS commands! I've forgotten every last one of them, but they were amazingly useful, and my productivity soared.

Moving to a mouse was a transformation and Windows98 and now WindowsXP, connected to the Internet, instant-messaging with the grandchildren, and conducting a writing and editing business with hardly ever needing to leave the house. Truly, the advance in technology has done exactly what it advertised: increased productivity and lowered cost in time, energy, and money.

Sure there are snags. The only reason we bought this most recent system, for example, is to increase compatibility with clients. As our computer guru tells us, "Software drives hardware. If you want to maintain maximum connectivity, you have to upgrade every four or five years." The upside of that necessity is the decrease in prices. Our two most recent systems are roughly equivalent. The one we bought in 1998 cost $2400. The one purchased in 2002 was just under a thousand.

We still don't have FAX at our house or high-speed Internet access or all the kinds of bells and whistles that folks have urged

Saturday's child works hard for a living.

us to consider. It turns out that, with technology as with most every issue in life, it's a judgment call, a kind of cost-benefit analysis. Is this the sort of change that will improve my life or not, and what sort of price must I pay, not only in money?

> *Thank you, Lord, for how incredibly many choices there are. Give us the energy and wisdom to make them wisely. Help us hold each alternative up to the light of your Christ and to see with your eyes. Amen.*

Sunday

*But the child born on the Sabbath day
is bright and blithe and bonny and gay.*

Playing Tangrams

MATTHEW 11:25 – 30

When I was growing up, we had a large volume of reproductions of Currier and Ives engravings. I poured over the pictures for hours, entranced by idealized Victorian images—liquid-eyed wives bidding adieux to their Union-soldier husbands, merry sledding parties bundled into horse-drawn sleighs, humble homesteads embowered with clouds of puffy pink apple blossoms.

Most of all, I was fascinated by the hidden picture puzzles in the back of the book. Nothing was what it at first seemed. A rock might turn into a man's face or a tree trunk hide a fox's head. The pictures worked on the principle of distraction. The artist made the illustration so busy you couldn't notice everything that was going on.

The Internet is a modern version of the picture puzzle. The screen is chock-a-block with images all vying for attention. We are bombarded with a constant flow of distractions. All claim equal importance. "Earthquake in Asia Minor"; "Fall Fashion Trends"; "Vote for your favorite candy flavor"; "Local News and

But the child born on the Sabbath day is bright and blithe and bonny and gay.

Weather." When we try to absorb the whole picture, we are overwhelmed by its complexity.

As I studied those Victorian engravings, I learned to find the hidden pictures. I discovered the only way was to clear the clutter and focus on one particular element at a time.

Modern life requires a similar tactic. We have to decide where to look first, and then determine if we are really seeing what we are looking at. As the puzzle pictures taught me, things are not always what they seem.

The world advances its busyness with complex puzzle pictures. Every day we are assailed by a myriad of choices about what to do, how to dress, where to go. The bright lights flash their vying advertisements encouraging us to Buy! Get! Try! Our heads spin and our eyes glaze. It's too much to take in. We're swamped with information, advertising, and just plain yakety-yak. God invites us to explore a completely different tack. God's solution is the calm and clarity of Sabbath rest.

An image I like to use in thinking of God's Sabbath is the ancient Chinese puzzle, the tangram. Tangrams make pictures by using the same seven pieces to construct hundreds of figures. Each problem is posed as a silhouette of the finished form, and one figures out how to use the seven pieces so they create the desired shape. There may be more than one way to solve the puzzle. There is one form but many solutions. These puzzles take "nothing" and make of it something. You get more with less.

God gave us the Sabbath for us to cool down and center ourselves from the frantic scurry of the week. It is an invitation to examine the pieces of our lives and reflect upon how successfully we are fitting them to our pattern, Jesus Christ. God's Sabbath is a foretaste of the wholeness, "at-one-ment," salvation

But the child born on the Sabbath day is bright and blithe and bonny and gay.

we are promised for eternity. The Sabbath is the day we are called to play tangrams with the fragments of our lives, putting them back together in conformity to Christ.

What a blessing for us to be invited one day a week to study the picture we are making from the pieces of our lives—spirit, family, self, work, money, relationships, recreation. Modern life is fractured and fragmented. There are many attractive pieces jumbled together in the box, but not all of them belong in our design. The Sabbath is a time to decide which pieces we truly value and what picture we want to be shaping.

> *In you, O God, we discover the wholeness
> of our minds, hearts, bodies, and spirits.
> We experience our unity with Christ Jesus, calling
> us to live focused more fully on you. Amen.*

We want to hear from you. Please send your comments about this book to us in care of the address below. Thank you.

ZONDERVAN™

GRAND RAPIDS, MICHIGAN 49530 USA

WWW.ZONDERVAN.COM